In Friendship

WHOSE WATER IS IT, ANYWAY?

TAKING WATER PROTECTION INTO PUBLIC HANDS

Maude Barlow

Published by ECW Press
665 Gerrard Street East
Toronto, Ontario, Canada M4M 1Y2
416-694-3348 / info@ecwpress.com

Editor for the Press: Susan Renouf
Cover design: Brienne Lim
Author photo: © Michelle Valberg
All photos courtesy the Council of Canadians,
except p. 91 © Ivars Kupcis/WCC.

LIBRARY AND ARCHIVES CANADA
CATALOGUING IN PUBLICATION

Title: Whose water is it, anyway? : taking
water protection into public hands /
Maude Barlow.

Names: Barlow, Maude, author.

Identifiers: Canadiana (print) 20190117257
Canadiana (ebook) 20190117265

ISBN 978-1-77041-430-3 (softcover)
ISBN 978-1-77305-428-5 (PDF)
ISBN 978-1-77305-427-8 (ePUB)

Subjects: LCSH: Blue Communities
Project. | LCSH: Water-supply. | LCSH:
Water-supply—Government policy. |
LCSH: Water resources development. |
LCSH: Water resources development—
Government policy. | LCSH: Water
security. | LCSH: Right to water.

Classification: LCC HD1691 .B37 2019
DDC 333.91—dc23

The publication of *Whose Water Is It Anyway?* is funded in part by the Government of Canada.
Ce livre est financé en partie par le gouvernement du Canada. We also acknowledge the contribution
of the Government of Ontario through the Ontario Book Publishing Tax Credit, and through
Ontario Creates for the marketing of this book.

 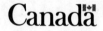

PRINTED AND BOUND IN CANADA   PRINTING: NORECOB   5 4 3 2 1

For Andrew, who is always there

TABLE OF CONTENTS

water crisis. With great warmth and precision, she also shows that by taking up the call for 'water justice' — so intimately connected to other struggles — we can start to build the society we want. This book has all the facts, forceful analysis and moral clarity that Canadians will need to wake up and join this most urgent of struggles." — NAOMI KLEIN, AUTHOR OF *THIS CHANGES EVERYTHING* AND *THE SHOCK DOCTRINE*

"*Boiling Point* is a rallying cry — a critical call to action."
— *HERIZONS MAGAZINE*

"Barlow concludes on a hopeful note, providing reasonable solutions that show how a 'blue and just Canada is possible.' She understands, however, that while most large corporations will do almost anything to increase profits, the primary responsibility for protecting citizens lies with governments at all levels. Barlow makes a convincing case that both our provincial and federal governments are failing this fundamental duty." — *VANCOUVER SUN*

"Barlow gives us more than a wakeup call. She gives us a call for action — now!" — CANADIAN ASSOCIATION OF LABOUR MEDIA

"As interest grows in water as a commodity, Barlow's book is timely and will resonate with environmentalists, those interested in international trade and anyone wondering just where Canada stands on the possible impending water crisis."
— *PUBLISHERS WEEKLY*

"Barlow's documentation of the very real threat to the global water supply is important reading as Canada faces key end-of-year deadlines regarding new pipeline development and meeting the targets of the Paris climate agreement." — *QUILL & QUIRE*

"*Boiling Point* is a concise, informative guide to Canada's water crisis . . . Here's hoping many Canadians read *Boiling Point* and demand the necessary action." — *THE UNITER*

INTRODUCTION

"All water has a perfect memory and is forever trying to get back to where it was." — TONI MORRISON

This is a book about hope.

It is a story about everyday people defending the water resources of their communities and protecting the broader human right to water by ensuring it is now and forever a public trust, one that must not be allowed to fall under private, for-profit control.

It is a story about a grassroots campaign to address the water crisis the world is facing, which counters the argument that the best way to address this crisis is to commodify water and let the market decide who gets access to it and how.

But it is not a story about naïveté. It faces head-on some deeply disturbing realities we must acknowledge if we are to move forward.

In May 2016, the UN Environment Programme (UNEP) released the most comprehensive environmental study the United Nations has ever undertaken. Reporting on its study's findings, UNEP called water scarcity the scourge of the Earth and linked it directly to humanity's continued degradation of the lands and forests that replenish the world's freshwater sources. In March 2018, UN Water released its annual World Water Development Report with a dire warning: if we do not change our ways, more than five billion people could suffer serious to severe water shortages in 30 years. Even today 3.6 billion people live in areas that are water scarce for at least a month per year. This could increase to as many as 5.7 billion people by 2050.

On top of these water shortages, there are many parts of the world where accessible, clean water is simply unavailable. An April 2017 report by the World Health Organization warned that at least two billion people worldwide drink water contaminated with feces every day, killing more than half a million people per year. WaterAid says that diarrhea caused by contaminated water and poor toilets kills a child under five every two minutes. The UN reports that 80% of wastewater from human activity is still discharged into waterways around the world without any pollution removal at all.

Some lay the blame for this at the feet of climate change.

While it is true that human-generated greenhouse gas emissions have affected the water cycle and natural water storage systems, it is equally true that our active, collective abuse of water is another major cause of the world's growing water crisis. Not only are we changing the climate around us as we heat up the world, we are polluting, depleting, damming, overextracting and diverting the planet's water systems. We are changing landscapes and local hydrologic cycles, creating deserts in some places and catastrophic floods in others. Communities already living without clean water because of poverty, inequality and discrimination now find themselves in further danger as local water sources dry up or are claimed for profit-related purposes.

Two populations are particularly affected by the global water crisis. In many places, women have the primary responsibility to provide water for their families and they must walk hours every day in their search. Often they bring along their girl children, who then miss school. Girls may also refuse to attend school if there are no proper and safe sanitation conditions. The United Nations reports that in sub-Saharan Africa alone, women collectively spend 200 million hours each day, or 40 billion hours a year, collecting water. In a world where more people have access to cell phones than toilets, women and girls living without a toilet collectively spend 266 million hours each day finding a place to go to the bathroom.

Indigenous Peoples around the world are also at extra risk from the water crisis. Often living in smaller and more remote communities, they have less collective power to stand up to large extractive industrial operations in their territories that damage their local water supplies. Along with peasants, many of them landless, and small rural farmers, Indigenous Peoples are the most marginalized and are particularly vulnerable to industrial pollution of their water sources and to a lack of proper sanitation. These factors, along with extreme poverty, deny them access to clean drinking water. This is not confined to the global South. Twice as many Native Americans live in poverty as the rest of the American population, and 7.5% of their homes do not have basic sanitation or safe drinking water. First Nations communities in Canada are 90% more likely not to have running water or toilets in their homes than the Canadian population in general.

In my previous books, I have asserted that to deal with this crisis, we need to work together to address both the ecological threat of a planet running out of accessible clean water and the deep injustice that these statistics reveal. It is also crucial to understand that the water crisis is not just taking place in poor countries but is a global issue now. Many industrialized countries are experiencing severe water shortages and the deep inequality that exists in the global South is increasingly being experienced in the wealthier countries of the global North.

This means that we can and must create a truly international movement to fight for water justice for all.

In my 2013 book, *Blue Future: Protecting Water for People and the Planet Forever*, I argued that a water-secure and water-just future depends on our adoption of four principles:

1. that water is a human right and is an issue of justice, not charity;
2. that water is a common heritage and public trust and therefore access to water must not be allowed to be decided by private, for-profit interests;
3. that water has rights beyond its service to humans and must be respected and protected for the ecosystem and other living beings; and
4. that, rather than being a source of conflict and division, water can be nature's gift to teach us how we might learn to live more lightly on the planet and in harmony with one another.

In some real ways, we have seen advances on some of the principles. After a long and gruelling fight, the majority of the countries that comprise the United Nations recognized that water and sanitation are fundamental human rights. Opposition to the takeover of municipal water services by private transnational water companies has grown, and there are many successful cases where municipalities have returned their water services to public management. Opposition to bottled water has also increased in the last few years, especially among the young, as people understand the heavy environmental footprint of this industry. And movements such as the Global Alliance for the Rights of Nature have sprung up around the world to promote the adoption of legal systems that recognize and enforce nature's own rights.

These are the benchmarks of progress on the macro scale, but there has been equivalent progress on a smaller and more local scale — the rise of the Blue Communities movement. In the last decade, an ever-growing number of municipalities and civil society institutions have designated themselves Blue Communities, committing to defend the human right to water and to help curb plastic contamination in their communities. It is an exciting and hopeful development, a crucial piece of the multi-faceted water-protection movement that is having real and positive results.

A Blue Community adopts three fundamental principles.

1. A Blue Community promises to protect and promote water and sanitation as human rights. This is in keeping with the United Nations' 2010 resolution declaring that water and sanitation are fundamental human rights and that no one should be denied these services because of an inability to pay.

2. A Blue Community promises to protect water as a public trust by promoting publicly financed, owned and operated water and wastewater services. All decisions about access to water and sanitation must be made by people and their elected officials, not by a for-profit investor.

3. Where there are accessible clean public water sources available, a Blue Community bans or phases out the sale of bottled water in municipal

facilities and at municipal events and promotes its tap water as a safe and reliable source of drinking water. While this step alone will not solve the planet's plastics crisis, it plays an important role in diminishing the devastating environmental footprint of the bottled water industry.

The Blue Communities project started in Canada in 2009 in reaction to the policies of the Conservative government then in power. Claiming that municipalities could save money, the federal government was promoting the privatization of Canadian water services by withholding federal funding to those towns and cities that refused to turn to a public-private partnership (P3) for water infrastructure upgrading. The Council of Canadians partnered with the Canadian Union of Public Employees and Eau Secours in Quebec to establish the Blue Communities project as a way of helping municipalities ward off unwanted privatization. To date, 27 Canadian municipalities have taken the Blue Communities pledge.

But the concept didn't stay in Canada. Surprising us initially, it started to catch on in other parts of the world: cities such as Bern, Paris, Thessaloniki and Berlin chose to become Blue Communities in highly visible, public ceremonies. Then it spread further. Institutions such as universities, unions and faith-based organizations adopted our principles and have also become Blue Communities, vowing to protect water and the human right to water in a variety of ways. Many find the concept empowering as it is a positive step forward in the face of the many environmental and human rights threats we now face.

For me, fighting for water justice has been a powerful personal journey. It has taken me from the United Nations and international conferences to the world's most terrible slums in search of the solution to the twin ecological and human water crises that threaten the planet and all living beings.

While I deeply believe that we need good and strong law at all levels of government to protect both ecosystems and humans from the coming global water crisis, the most powerful actions we can take personally are at the local level.

This book reflects a dream of a world going Blue, one community at a time.

CHAPTER ONE

The Fight Against Corporate Control of Water

My obsession with water started in 1985. Brian Mulroney was the newly minted Canadian prime minister, a political ally of both U.S. president Ronald Reagan and British prime minister Margaret Thatcher, the chief cheerleaders of economic globalization and its pro-corporate policies of privatization, deregulation and free trade. One of the first things that Prime Minister Mulroney did upon taking office was to address a gathering of blue-chip business elite at the Economic Club in New York City. There he announced that Canada was "open for business" and praised President Reagan, promising new military cooperation between the two countries and an end to restrictions on American investment in Canada.

So, it was no surprise that Reagan and Mulroney soon announced they were negotiating the Canada-U.S. Free Trade Agreement, the first of the modern free trade deals and the model for the later North American Free Trade Agreement (NAFTA), the World Trade Organization and thousands of other bilateral trade and investment agreements between countries. Unlike free trade agreements of the past, this one would be less about taking down tariffs on the trade in goods — which were largely gone anyway — and more about establishing an integrated North American market where borders would be largely eliminated and governments would step aside on matters of business.

Ronald Reagan was deep into his agenda of increased military spending, deregulation of environmental protections, tax cuts to the wealthy and corporations and promoting the majority Judeo-Christian worldview. Fearing that a free trade agreement would give Reagan the power to challenge Canadian social security, foreign and resource policy, many of us in the Canadian social-justice movement came together to oppose it. We formed the Council of Canadians to promote independent social, resource, cultural and foreign policy for Canada and to resist the right-wing agenda of the Reagan administration. One area of particular sensitivity was whether this proposed trade deal would give Americans access to Canada's resources, especially energy and water. The latter was an issue I was beginning to monitor as fights over access to Canada's water reserves were heating up.

While reading the massive text that was the proposed free trade agreement, I stumbled upon the Annex, the material at the end of the agreement that listed all the goods to be covered and therefore subject to its rules. To my complete surprise, the Annex listed "water, including . . . mineral waters . . . ice and snow." Since the trade deal had made it clear that no signatory country could restrict the trade or export of any of the listed goods, alarm bells went off in my head and heart. Over a number of generations, various plans had surfaced to sell massive amounts of water to the U.S. through pipelines, aqueducts, tunnels and dams. But Canadians had, until then, successfully held off these gambits to commodify our water resources. That this had reared its head again — that the commercialization of water exports could be allowed and protected by a free trade agreement — frightened me and set me on a path of discovery.

I would turn out to be right that this and other free trade agreements indeed pose a grave threat to both the public control of water and water protection itself, but it was a number of years before that became evident.

Meanwhile, I asked myself, *Who owns water and who is making decisions about this precious resource?* I had always assumed that water belongs to us all. But I was about to learn that the world was straining its water resources even then and that a number of private corporations and interests were moving in to take control of and profit from growing water scarcity. I was setting out on a journey of discovery at the very time that the commodification of the world's water was beginning in a serious way.

Privatization of water services

In the late 1980s, Great Britain's prime minister Margaret Thatcher sold off the public water utilities of England and Wales as part of her government cutbacks initiative. Household water rates have soared more than 40% since then, and the corporations that had taken over the management of water services became infamous for their terrible record of pollution, astronomical CEO salaries and bonuses and their annual massive tax avoidance schemes. Thirty years later, the private water companies operating in Britain have paid out billions to their shareholders, as reported in a June 2017 *Independent* story, while deliberately racking up public debt to finance profits. They made a combined total post-tax profit of almost US$25 billion over the last ten years. At the time, however, water privatization was seen as a daring new frontier of economic globalization that would save governments money. Thatcher's experiment started a domino effect of water privatization schemes around the world.

The World Bank quickly jumped into the fray: water privatization became a condition for funding poor countries in the global South. This was part of a "structural adjustment" program designed to bring these countries into a global market economy by privatizing essential services in exchange for debt relief. Over the course of the 1990s, the World Bank and other regional development banks dramatically increased the number of loans they assigned based on an agreement by the recipient country to move to a private system of water management and delivery. In many cases, the banks chose the private water utility — often the water divisions of two French giants, Suez Environment and Veolia Water — and even signed the contracts, leaving the local governments out of the equation altogether.

Major institutions started to refer to water as a commodity. At a 1992 conference held in Dublin, the United Nations for the first time declared that water has an "economic value" in its "competing uses" and that it should be recognized as an "economic good." This definition is one used by the private sector to promote private water delivery and was the first signal that the UN would open the door to defining water as a commodity rather than a commons. Suez and Veolia joined the UN Global Compact — a contentious initiative that encourages some of the worst polluting corporations to adopt voluntary environmental and human rights standards — and soon entrenched themselves in the drafting of the 2000 UN Millennium Development Goals.

In 1993, the World Bank tabled a new policy that referred to the "unwillingness" of the poor to pay for water services and stated that water should be treated as an economic commodity with an emphasis on efficiency, financial discipline and full-cost recovery. The intent was to guarantee that private water corporations investing in poor countries would recover both the cost of their investment and enough money to give their investors a profit by raising water rates as needed.

And new institutions were born. The World Water Council, which calls itself an international water policy think tank, was formed in 1997 to promote the interests of private water companies. It is sponsored by the World Bank and some agencies and interests of the United Nations, giving it great credibility. All the big private water utilities are founding members, as well as many invest-ment banks and the International Water Association that has more than 500 corporate members. Every three years, the World Water Council holds the World Water Forum, a gathering that serves as a showcase for the private water sector. Thousands of government officials come from all over the world to attend and learn about all the "benefits" of water privatization.

In 2008, the World Bank also created the 2030 Water Resources Group to advise it on water policy in the global South and how to implement the UN Sustainable Development Goal on water. Its partners include the major water service corporations, such as Suez; the big bottled water companies, Nestlé, Coca-Cola, and PepsiCo; beer giants, such as Anheuser-Busch; and chemical companies, such as Dow. All are major transnational corporations that privatize, commodify, deplete and pollute the planet's water. They are given authenticity by the fact that the World Bank, the United Nations Development Programme and the World Economic Forum (the outfit that invites corporate and government elites to Davos, Switzerland, every year) are also founding members of the 2030 Water Resources Group.

This history of water services privatization has been well documented. To make their profit goals, private water companies cut corners on water quality protection, delivery of services and investing in source water protection. They routinely raise water rates even when they have signed a contract to keep rates at a certain level, and on average they lay off one in three water workers when they take over a public facility.

The public and their communities lose when local government officials turn over the responsibility for and control of this vital public service. Private water companies are accountable to their shareholders, not to the people they serve, and they often restrict public access to information about their operations.

Private water services charge more. In a 2016 study, Washington, D.C.–based Food & Water Watch reported that privately owned water utilities charged 59% more for drinking water services and 63% more for sewage services than public utilities.

Although there has been fierce opposition to the privatization of water services, the companies continue to grow as they expand into new markets in countries such as India, Brazil and China. According to their websites, the water divisions of the two biggest transnational water corporations, Suez and Veolia, collectively employ 250,000 people and cleared profits of more than US$60 billion in 2017.

Rising water rates

The privatization of water services is contributing to the rise in water tariffs around the world, which in turn is leading to cut-offs to households that cannot pay their bills. Global Water Intelligence is the leading publisher of the international private water industry; in its October 2017 annual report on global water rates, the group announced that water tariffs around the world are growing at twice the global rate of inflation.

In the U.S., according to a May 2017 survey done by Circle of Blue, a non-profit network of journalists and scientists who cover water issues, water rates have increased by 54% since 2010 and are becoming so onerous that as many as one-third of Americans may be unable to pay their monthly water bill.

Food & Water Watch reports that over the last 15 years, water bills in the U.S. have increased at three times the rate of inflation, whereas household incomes have fallen by more than US$3,500 per household between 2000 and 2014 according to the U.S. Census Bureau. This has made low-income Americans vulnerable. In *America's Secret Water Crisis*, published in October 2018, the group reported that, at a conservative estimate, at least 15 million people in the U.S. experienced water shut-offs in 2016. Detroit, Michigan, has cut off water services to tens of thousands of residents in the last several years, mostly to the poor, the unemployed and African-Americans, who together make up around 83% of the population.

In poor countries, water cut-offs inevitably affect the most vulnerable first. During the severe 2014–2017 water shortage in São Paulo, Brazil, the residents of the favelas, already living in a day-to-day scramble to find clean water, were hit first and hardest. Water is not delivered to individual households but often through a single pipe to the whole community. Reduced water flows can mean no water at all for a community. But where water has been restricted to the whole city, the wealthy can afford to pay for private water sources.

Even families with indoor plumbing are vulnerable. I toured a working-class suburb in São Paulo at the height of the drought and met families that had bored holes in their basement in search of water. They had running water only twice a day for an hour, once at six o'clock in the morning and then again at ten o'clock at night. The quality of the water coming from their taps was often not safe.

The scene is set for a perfect storm: depleting clean water sources around the world, growing poverty and inequality among countries and within countries and rising water rates that put the price of water out of the reach of millions.

Plastic water

As I was learning and monitoring and writing about all of this, another source of water commodification took off. Bottled water is not new, of course, but it was initially created for the wealthy and served in glass bottles. What started as an upscale consumer product, mostly confined to Europe, became one of the fastest-growing industries in the world.

In the 1970s, about one billion litres of water were sold annually. By 2017, that number had risen to 391 billion litres and, according to Transparency Market Research, global annual bottled water consumption will reach 465 billion litres by 2020 with sales topping US$300 billion. Most bottled water is now sold in plastic bottles. A new trend in Latin America is selling water-filled small plastic bags — sold by the hundreds in large plastic bags — that people can just keep in their pockets so that they can be "hydrated" at any time.

Nestlé Waters is the number-one bottled water company in the world. Created in 1992, Nestlé has almost 34,000 employees in 34 countries and owns 49 distinct brands, such as Poland Spring, San Pellegrino, Perrier and Nestlé Pure Life, the largest bottled water brand worldwide. Nestlé Waters reports that its annual sales in 2017 amounted to almost US$8 billion.

The water divisions of other major companies, such as Coca-Cola's Dasani and Smartwater and PepsiCo's Aquafina, are growing so fast that, in 2016, they outpaced soft drink sales in the U.S. for the first time.

The bottled water industry defends itself from criticism by arguing that it uses less water overall than other large raw water users, such as agribusinesses. But the water they use to bottle and sell is taken from individual springs and wells and can deplete large local areas of water.

In 2000, Coca-Cola opened a bottling plant in Plachimada in the southern Indian state of Kerala. Over the next few years, local farmers noted that their groundwater supply was drying up and what was left was contaminated. I had the privilege of sitting for several mornings, back in 2004, with local village women who had been holding a protest vigil outside the plant every day for three years. Eventually their protest was successful: the plant was ordered to shut down three years later. To this day, the villagers say they have had no compensation for the loss of their livelihoods. Four more Coca-Cola bottled water plants in India have since been forced to close down as local communities faced severe water shortages.

Citizens in tiny Osceola Township in Michigan are in a battle to stop Nestlé from expanding its water-takings operation to 1,600 litres per minute from its current 900 litres. Already, reports a February 2018 Agence France-Presse story, residents say the local environment is being damaged by Nestlé's Ice Mountain plant and point to a dramatic drop in water levels of the town's Twin Creek River. Town manager Tim Ladd said that one doesn't have to be a geologist or a hydrologist to see how the water levels are affected. The community is particularly incensed that Nestlé pays just US$200 a year to the state of Michigan to pump out more than 520 million litres of its local water that it then seals in plastic and ships away.

Vittel, France, is home to Vittel Bonne Source, one of the world's most popular mineral waters. It has been operating since the 1850s, but many residents now want no more to do with the business. The brand has been owned by Nestlé since the early 1990s and currently bottles a billion litres of water per year, or two million bottles per day, from the groundwater beneath Vittel. The local water table is sinking as a result, according to an April 2018 story in *The Telegraph*. An investigation by the French government's geologic bureau found that the groundwater levels have been falling by 30 centimetres per year since 1990 and are down ten metres in the last four decades. If nothing is done to halt the water loss, the town may have to pipe in water from another village at a cost of over US$56 million. Residents know that they will pay for this with higher water rates.

Residents of Sululta, Ethiopia, cannot reconcile why half their population has to walk miles to find water from muddy wells when their area is booming with industry; the Abyssinia Springs bottled water plant and four other bottled water companies have access to so much water. As a May 2017 *Guardian* story reports, the situation is particularly galling because the town is situated in the highlands where rainfall is abundant. In fact, the government refers to Ethiopia as the "water tower of Africa." Abyssinia Springs, of which Nestlé owns a majority stake, pumps 50,000 litres an hour, while many residents must pay for contaminated water at private wells or walk great distances for free but unsafe water. Lack of access to clean water and other basic public services led to an uprising in November 2015. Human rights groups report that at least 600 people were killed by state security forces.

In a November 2013 media release, corporate watchdog SumOfUs reported that about a decade before, Nestlé launched an aggressive water grab in water-starved Pakistan. It said the people of the small Punjab village of Bhati Dilwan have watched their water table sink hundreds of metres since Nestlé started pumping its groundwater for its Pure Life bottled water. The children are getting sick from the foul-smelling sludge they are forced to choke down after the water from the shallow local wells is gone.

Fiji, a premium bottled water found in upscale hotels

and restaurants all over the world, is named for the South Pacific archipelago from which it's sourced. In a 2012 in-depth investigation of the operation, *Mother Jones*'s Anna Lenzer pointed out that there are two types of water available on the island: the expensive type you can buy in a plastic bottle and what comes out of the tap, the latter being all that is available to the majority of the residents who are poor. The tap water comes through broken and contaminated water pipes and carries typhoid and gastroenteritis bacteria; the local people regularly suffer outbreaks of typhoid and parasitic infections. Lenzer also uncovered the fact that the company's signature bottle is made from Chinese plastic in a diesel-fueled plant and hauled thousands of kilometres to Fiji where it's filled with Fiji water and then shipped around the world.

On top of the harmful impacts the bottled water industry has on local communities, their water supplies and their human rights, it also packs an enormous environmental footprint. In 2009, American scientists Peter Gleick and H.S. Cooley from California's Pacific Institute published a study called *Energy Implications of Bottled Water*. Based on bottled water sales at that time, the authors concluded that the energy needed to make the plastic bottles; process the water that goes into them; and clean, fill, seal, label and transport them to market was the equivalent of about 160 million barrels of oil — up to 2,000 times the energy required to produce the equivalent volume of tap water. Our addiction to bottled water, wrote the authors, was then pumping about 20 million metric tons of carbon dioxide into the atmosphere every year

— equivalent to the monthly output of 20 million homes. Since bottled water consumption has more than doubled since this study was released, the industry's energy footprint will also have risen commensurately.

And then there is the plastics nightmare. An exclusive June 2017 bombshell report by *The Guardian* revealed that a million plastic bottles are bought around the world every minute, a figure predicted to jump dramatically in the next few years. Citing Euromonitor International's global packaging trend report, the newspaper goes on to say that the world will be producing half a trillion plastic bottles every year by 2020. While some soft drinks come in plastic, by far the biggest culprit is bottled water, and the spread of its Western "on the go" culture to China and the Asia Pacific region. If placed end to end, the number of single-use plastic bottles now sold each year would extend more than halfway to the sun.

A stunning 91% of all plastic bottles do not get recycled; since plastic takes more than 400 years to degrade, most of these bottles are somewhere on the planet, wrote *National Geographic* in a July 2017 special report. Many end up in landfills or in lakes and rivers. And many have found their way into the world's oceans, where they join plastic trash from other sources to form five massive plastic garbage patches known as gyres. We are dumping so much plastic into our oceans, according to research by the Ellen MacArthur Foundation, that by 2050 they will contain more plastic by weight than fish. The planet's beaches and islands, even in the Arctic and in remote areas, are being overrun by this blight.

In March 2019, multiple media sources carried the story of a dead whale that washed ashore in the Philippines with almost 40 kilograms of plastic waste in its stomach. The plastic was so compact, it was calcified. A whale found in Spain in February 2019 had 29 kilograms of plastics in its stomach and another dead whale that washed up on the shores of Indonesia in November 2018 had ingested more than 1,000 pieces of plastic, including plastic bags, 115 plastic drinking cups and two pairs of flip-flops.

Greenpeace reports that Coca-Cola alone produces more than 100 billion throwaway plastic bottles every year — 3,400 per second. The industry could, if it chose, use recycled plastic known as rPET, says Greenpeace, but the top six bottled water companies in the world use a combined average of just 6.6% of this recycled plastic in their products. None have plans to use only recycled plastic across their global production.

Scientists have confirmed that people who eat seafood ingest tiny pieces of plastic. *National Geographic* reports that micro-plastics have been found in birds and fish and whales, drinking water, beer, table salt and 114 aquatic species. In October 2018, the magazine reported that for the first time, micro-plastics had been found in human stool and posed this troubling question: once inside the human body, can plastic nano-fibres — some five times smaller than the width of a human hair — work their way into the human bloodstream, lymphatic system or even reach a person's liver?

And it's not just in open waterways and tap water. A recent global study found micro-plastics in 93% of the bottled water tested around the world. As reported by the CBC in March 2018, the U.S.-based non-profit journalism organization Orb Media tested the bottled water of 11 major brands, including Nestlé Pure Life, Aquafina, Dasani, Evian and San Pellegrino. Almost all contained some sort of micro-plastic, including polypropylene, polystyrene, nylon and polyethylene terephthalate (PET). On average, there were 10.4 particles of plastic per litre that were 100 microns (0.10 mm) or bigger. This is twice the level of micro-plastics as in tap water, which the group tested from more than a dozen countries across all five continents.

Our addiction to bottled water has come home to haunt us.

The many faces of water commodification

My initial interest in the question of how free trade deals like NAFTA put our water at risk broadened as I began to comprehend the interconnected nature of the human right to water and the need to protect water in its natural state. I realized that the more we mistreated water, overextracting and polluting it, the less there would be left to divide up fairly. And when there is not enough to go around, the most vulnerable are hurt first and most. Understanding this inter-connectedness helped harden my resolve to fight against private control of the planet's water in its many forms.

The privatization of municipal water services and the bottled water industry are only two of the many and growing forms of water commodification taking place around the world.

Water trading, sometimes called water rights, is the commercial exchange of water entitlements where water has been separated from the land and is bought and sold as a commodity.

In 1981, Chilean dictator Augusto Pinochet introduced a draconian Water Code that allowed water property privatization and the separation of land control from water control. This opened the door for the unrestrained purchase and sale of water, transforming it into a market asset and granting the new "owners" unlimited water rights for free and in perpetuity. As Sara Larraín of the environmental organization Chile Sustentable explains in her 2012 report, *Human Rights and Market Rules in Chile's Water Conflicts*, once water rights are given away, the government no longer intervenes and the reallocation of water happens by means of a water market: private owners of water rights can rent, buy or sell them, as with any other private asset. The ownership of Chile's water became concentrated in the hands of the hydroelectric, mining and agribusiness export sectors.

Seventy-five percent of all mineral production in the country is in the hands of private companies, most of them foreign owned. Additionally, three private companies own more than 90% of the water rights for power generation for the whole country. And the agricultural sector consumes nearly 85% of all water granted nationwide, with the bulk of the crops grown for export. As transnational mining, agribusiness and other companies took control of Chile's water sources, local villages, peasant communities, farmers and Indigenous Peoples were left bereft of water. Sara Larraín further points out that the agribusiness exporters rely heavily on pesticides, herbicides and fertilizers to produce their crops, and they appear not to be concerned about the pollution and overuse legacy they leave behind.

On the other side of the world, Australia created its water market in 1993, hoping that the ability to sell excess water would encourage farmers to conserve. While 65% of the Murray-Darling Basin is withheld to protect the environment, a volume of water estimated to be worth about US$11 billion remains available for trade on the water commodity market. Unwittingly, the government unleashed a free-for-all in which water brokers, unhampered by regulation, have since bought and sold water at exorbitant prices.

In 2000, water sold for AU$2 per megalitre; by 2014, the price had risen to AU$1,500 per megalitre; and by 2018, private premium water was selling for as much as AU$2,500 per megalitre. In a November 2017 story, Australian business magazine *INTHEBLACK* published a story on water investor David Williams, calling him one of a new breed of "water barons" who have become wealthy from water trading. Unashamed, Williams prefers to call himself a "water bandit." Several years ago, he invested AU$10 million in a water rights scheme in Tasmania, and today his profit grows at a rate of 20% per year. Australia is now officially in permanent drought, says the government. The value of William's private water stash will make him and other water barons richer in the coming years.

While these may appear to be isolated examples, water trading is prevalent in North America and being promoted in some water-scarce European countries, including Spain. In the American west, water rights were created in the 19th century and granted right into the early 20th century to entice settlers, ranchers and miners from the east with the promise of perpetual access to large amounts of water. Called "first in time first in use," these water rights are passed on from generation to generation. In recent years, a number of entitlement holders have started to trade their water rights, thereby profiting from local droughts. Large farmers in California are selling their water allocations to new developments and industries, and Texan billionaire T. Boone Pickens is selling water he bought from the threatened Ogallala Aquifer to private water suppliers.

Large multinational mining and oil companies also use negotiated water rights to commodify the resource when they gain access to local water sources through contracts with the local governments often, but not always, in the global South. These companies often acquire decades worth of water and tax concessions as governments are desperate to attract foreign investment.

In 2010, under the terms of NAFTA, the Canadian government was required to pay $131 million to an American forest products company for the water rights it left behind when it abandoned its 100-year-old Newfoundland pulp and paper operation without warning. And just two years later, the federal government amended the Fisheries Act to allow mining companies to have local lakes re-designated as "tailings impoundment areas," so they could dump their toxic waste without being subject to environmental protection laws. In essence, this process privatized whole lakes for mining companies' use.

Mining consumes and pollutes a great deal of water. Vast amounts are needed for drilling and washing the minerals, and because chemicals must often be added in the extraction process (such as cyanide in gold mining or arsenic in uranium mining), it causes significant pollution. Beyond these polluting additives, the runoff from drilling and washing is itself contaminated. Often, these factors cause conflict with local communities whose need for water comes second to the demands of industry.

Hundreds of gold and copper mines have opened in the last few years to meet the world's soaring demand for these minerals, used in the manufacture of electronic devices, according to a July 2017 article in *The Guardian*. Guatemala has awarded more than 350 new mining licences since 2007, mostly to Canadian companies, and another 600 are under consideration. Where there were only 17 mining operations in the Philippines in 1997, there are now nearly 50 mega-mines operating there.

Almost everywhere these mega-mines operate, there are conflicts over water and the control the industry has over local water sources. Philippe Sibaud is a trustee with the Gaia Foundation and the author of several major reports on the human rights abuses of the mining industry. He says that across Latin America, Asia and Africa, rivers and ecosystems are falling under foreign mining companies' control and the rights of local farmers and Indigenous communities are being ignored.

In my travels in the global South, I came upon another

pernicious form of water theft — water and land grabbing. Land grabs involve governments or agribusiness investors buying up huge parcels of land in their own or other countries either to feed their own populations or to export the food for profit. The Worldwatch Institute estimates that land at least three times the size of Great Britain has been acquired by wealthy agribusiness investors in poor countries. Many leases are for decades — some for as long as 99 years. But land grabs are not restricted to poor countries. Saudi Arabian agribusiness and dairy companies are buying up large tracts of land in California and Arizona to grow alfalfa to feed their farm animals back home, as the country does not have sufficient water resources itself.

Saudi Arabia and China — another major land grabber — know that land grabs are also water grabs, as the land bought or leased comes with its water sources. Not only do the investors choose prime agricultural land but they also tie up local surface and groundwater sources, displacing the locals who have traditionally relied on the land and its water. These agribusinesses bring mechanized, flood-irrigated, chemical-dependent, large-scale food production methods with them wherever they operate, often in water-scarce parts of the world where small-scale and dry-land farming is the only viable method for the local climate.

Water grabbing's sister is virtual water — the water used to produce manufactured goods, from clothes to computers, and embedded in agricultural products from beef to wheat to rice. Much of these activities is water intensive, and the water used to produce these goods or foods is "consumed," meaning it is not returned to the watershed. When the commodity is exported, or even moved to a different part of the country, the water is exported too. Virtual water is the way most water is moved around the world, even though when people think about water exports, they think of raw water moving through pipelines, aqueducts and canals.

Many wealthy countries conserve their own water supplies by importing water-intensive commodities. While in some cases, products such as bananas and coffee cannot be produced in colder climates and so are imported, increasingly countries are using the land and water of others to provide staples they could grow. When a country imports one kilogram of wheat instead of producing it domestically, for instance, it is saving about 1,350 litres of its own water sources. While in theory, the trade in virtual water could allow commodities produced in water-rich countries to be exported to countries with fewer water supplies, the reality is that wealthy countries are able to maintain their own water security by growing food in other countries and importing it.

Often virtual water is exported from areas that are land rich but water poor, using limited water supplies for export commodities. This is the story of California, where the traditional water rights allotments give large-scale agribusiness access to cheap water. In this way, the state is able to produce and export many water-intensive commodities, from wine to flowers, most of the world's almonds and large amounts of alfalfa. Australia, the world's driest inhabited continent, is a leading exporter of virtual water, shipping away its water in rice, wine and cotton.

The land grabs in Africa and other water-stressed regions of the global South are particularly distressing, however, as they displace local farmers, peasants and sometimes even whole communities. American hedge funds now control food production in a number of African countries. While China and India displace their own rural farmers and communities to make way for free trade zones and commercial development, they are also investing heavily in Africa to meet the food demands of their growing populations and the consumer demands of their emerging wealthy class. All of this puts unprecedented stress on the continent's water supplies.

The world's leading expert on virtual water is Arjen Y. Hoekstra, who teaches at the University of Twente in the Netherlands and is the supervisory board chair of the Water Footprint Network. Hoekstra says that if we include the virtual water we eat in our food and in other products we consume, the global per capita water footprint is 4,000 litres of water per day — ten to twelve times higher than the figure normally cited by the UN and other agencies. In his groundbreaking 2012 study, *The Water Footprint of Humanity*, Hoekstra linked the overextraction of the Earth's water sources to free trade. He found that more than one-fifth of the world's water supply goes to crops and commodities produced for export. Free trade agreements are another process by which water is commodified, and they are closely linked to the trade in virtual water.

Modern free trade and investment agreements commodify water in a number of ways. Water is considered a tradable good subject to the commercial rules of trade, as

I'd first learned in 1985 reading the alarming Annex eventually adopted in the North American Free Trade Agreement. That definition has been carried forward into other trade and investment agreements signed since. If a government attempts to interfere with a commercial agreement to sell water from one country to another, it could be challenged by the rules of trade that limit the ability of governments to interfere with trade of the identified "goods."

Most modern free trade agreements also contain enforceable rights for investors. The provision is called investor-state dispute settlement (ISDS), and it gives foreign corporations and investors the right to challenge governments if they introduce any new laws — be they related to environmental, health or workers' rights — or interpret any existing law in a way that would cause the investor to lose money. The corporation can sue that country's government for financial compensation. There are now more than 3,500 bilateral deals around the world that contain ISDS, and corporations have used the provision well over 900 times to sue governments. The majority of decisions have favoured the corporations, reports the United Nations Conference on Trade and Development.

Under NAFTA, Mexico and Canada have paid millions of dollars to American corporations unhappy with rules that protect the environment and water. These include a ban on cross-border trade in PCBs, a moratorium on fracking in a fragile area of a major river and a ban on the pesticide 2,4-D. In late 2018, an American coal mining company announced a NAFTA ISDS challenge of $1.4 billion against the province of Alberta for phasing out of coal-fired energy generation.

Free trade deals favour privatization of services. A public service may be exempted and protected when the deal is signed, but if a government later privatizes its service, it becomes difficult to bring it back under public management. Absurdly, it is then seen as a form of expropriation of the rights of the foreign for-profit company operating the service. If a municipality decides to enter into a public-private partnership to run its water services, for example, it must open up the competition to foreign and domestic private water utilities. If it has awarded the contract to a foreign company but several years later decides it has made a mistake and tries to bring its water services back under public management, the company can use ISDS to sue for compensation.

Water pollution trading is another form of water commodification. It replaces regulations and fines with a system that allows companies to pay or trade to continue to pollute. Water pollution trading promotes "environmental markets" by allowing a company to exceed its allowable pollution level through the purchase of credit from another company or operation that has not exceeded its limit. In a November 2015 report, the legal team at Food & Water Watch said that water pollution trading gives more control to polluters, opens the door to water trading brokers and reduces democratic control over local water. They report in disturbing detail how large polluters, like factory farms, have found new ways to get around the law. Not only has water pollution trading not improved water quality in the United States where it is in place, but it has also undermined the Clean Water Act.

A mighty contest

In the years since I set out on this journey of discovery, the concept of water as a natural resource belonging to all has changed, as the world has gone through a profound political metamorphosis. While it is true that water has been used for centuries — often ruthlessly — as a tool for industrial development, it was always assumed to be endless in supply. As nations grew wealthy, their people held that governments had a responsibility to provide essential services such as universal education, health care and clean water for all. Universal access to water is standard in many parts of the industrialized world. Even in countries where the poor, the marginalized and those discriminated against based on race, religion or caste did not have equal access to water, the stated goal of governments was to eventually provide water for all. But the notion of universal rights was soon questioned by a ruthless political and economic narrative where everything became up for grabs.

With the advent of economic globalization in the late 1970s, most governments and international institutions bought into an economic and development model based on the belief that markets should be able to rule themselves — that what is good for the market is good for us all. The model includes limits on the role of governments, the privatization of public services, deregulation of environmental and other "red tape" rules, free trade agreements that favour corporations and tax breaks for the wealthy and corporations in the nation-state competition for investment.

In those years, many nation-state companies became

multinational corporations. They outgrew their domestic market and took their technological know-how and the backing of the rules of economic globalization to shift their production to low-wage parts of the world where environmental rules were nonexistent or not enforced. With time, as some grew very large, they became transnational corporations — entities that transcended their country of origin. Another term for the corporate giants is metanationals, companies that are essentially stateless and in effect vie for power with the nation-states of the world. Metanationals might have legal domicile in one country, corporate management in another, financial assets in a third and administrative and production staff scattered all over.

Transnational corporations also hide their profits in tax havens, robbing governments of revenues needed for social programs and infrastructure. The U.K.-based group Tax Justice calls this practice "profit shifting" and reported in March 2017 that, based on figures from the UN University World Institute for Development Economics Research, the global loss of tax revenues exceeds US$500 billion a year.

A 2016 study of the 100 top economies in the world found that 69 were corporations, up from 63 the previous year, and only 31 were countries. The U.K. anti-poverty organization Global Justice Now reported that the ten biggest corporations, including Walmart, Apple and Shell, make more money than most of the countries of the world combined. Walmart is bigger than Spain, Australia and the Netherlands; Royal Dutch Shell is bigger than Mexico and Sweden; Toyota is bigger than India, Belgium and Russia; Berkshire Hathaway is bigger than Saudi Arabia.

In the journal *Foreign Policy*, international relations expert Parag Khanna writes that this development is not just about new ways of making money; it also unsettles the definition of a "global superpower" as the world enters an era in which the most powerful law is not that of sovereignty but that of supply and demand.

In this new world, the resources needed to feed the insatiable demands of these corporations become vital, and controlling access to them even more so. Soil and forests and minerals and energy are all essential to the global economy. So too is water. International food justice activist and scientist Vandana Shiva says the speculative economy of global finance is hundreds of times larger than the value of real goods and services produced in the world. Financial capital is hungry for investments and returns on investments. In order for it to succeed, it must commodify everything on the planet, she explains — land and water, plants and genes, microbes and mammals.

Water is increasingly viewed as a market commodity to be bought and sold on the open market, backed by such powerful institutions as the World Bank and parts of the United Nations, as well as many political leaders. Decisions are being made all the time about scarce water sources: should they be used to provide water to villagers, small farmers and communities or should the water be allocated to free trade zones, industrial parks and centres for high technology? In many institutions, industries and governments, water is seen as "blue gold" and captured by private interests.

In addition to these methods of water commodification, private companies own and operate many of the dams, infrastructure, nanotechnology, desalination plants and water purification systems that governments are looking to for technological solutions to their water crises. Private companies are buying up land and water to control the growing biofuel industry. Private companies partner with governments to lay the pipes and infrastructure for water systems around the world. Private companies dump their waste into public waters, essentially commodifying them as they are no longer accessible to the local populace. Banks, pension funds and global investment firms have set up portfolios so that ordinary investors can reap the benefits of water commodification.

Many major banks and stock market companies are creating and enlarging their water portfolios. James McWhinney is an American mutual fund consultant whose writing appears in the online investment journal *Investopedia*. In a blog published in February 2018, McWhinney acknowledges that water is the source of life but that its scarcity also makes it a great area for portfolio diversification and lists some of the major indexes designed to track water-related investment opportunities: the Dow Jones U.S. Water Index, with a market capitalization of US$150 million; the ISE B&S Water Index, containing more than 35 different stocks; the S&P Global Water Index, made up of 50 companies in the water business, and many others.

Global Water Intelligence (GWI), the leading publisher of reports and research for the international private water market, published a report in August 2018 that predicted a rosy future for water markets. In 2018, said the report, the value of the global water market was US$770 billion but was set to expand to US$915 billion by 2023. GWI publisher Christopher Gasson explained that the global water market is growing faster than it has since 2010 and is driven by a recovering global economy, major water infrastructure plans around the world, an increase in global mining activities, new desalination projects and a growing global commodities market. But he also linked strong water markets with the recovery of oil prices and increasing fossil fuel production, including fracking, and noted the many ways water is needed in the production of fossil fuel energy.

In other words, the growth in fossil fuels, mining and industrial farming — all major causes of the planet's water crisis — is great for investors.

No wonder business schools around the world teach their students that the only way to solve the global water crisis is to treat it like oil and gas and let the market decide its price and worth. What they usually don't discuss is who and how many will have to do without water when the ruthless market they have created puts the price of water beyond the reach of untold millions.

CHAPTER TWO

The Creation of a Global Water Justice Movement

Building a global water justice movement to counter the commodification of water has been a labour of love for me and the thousands of other "water warriors" around the world fighting to protect water and all of life, which depends on it. And it is a real David and Goliath story.

After discovering in the 1980s that water was considered a tradable good in trade agreements and accepted as an economic good by the United Nations, I read everything I could get my hands on, but there was little in the way of analysis at that time. There was plenty of excellent research on the impact of structural adjustment programs in the global South: how poor countries were being forced to adopt neo-liberal economic policies in exchange for debt relief or funding from the World Bank and other regional development banks. But it was not until Thatcher privatized Great Britain's water services and the World Bank launched its water privatization projects as part of its structural adjustment program that we could connect the dots.

In 1994, I was invited to the founding meeting of the International Forum on Globalization (IFG) in San Francisco, a gathering of groundbreaking thinkers and activists fighting to counter the policies of economic globalization. One of the key issues was how the politics of privatization, deregulation and free trade were affecting communities around the world. We looked at the impacts this political trend was having on their access to and control of their local resources, be they soil, forests, minerals or water, the basic things they needed to survive. This was the perfect place from which to launch an inquiry, and in 2001 the IFG published my first report on water called *Blue Gold: The World Water Crisis and the Commodification of the World's Water Supply.* We translated the report into several languages and sent it out to the world. The response was incredible.

We heard from communities all over the world who were fighting water service privatization schemes, bottled water operations, transnational mining companies and others gaining access to their water sources through government contracts. I personally went on to write other books and many reports on water, but the reaction to this first report told me that we who were concerned needed to find one another — and do it fast.

Crashing their party

The World Water Council (WWC), which promotes the interests of private water companies, was launched and held its first small forum in March 1997 in Marrakech, Morocco. But its first large public forum took place in March 2000 in The Hague and was attended by more than 6,000 people; its concurrent water fair was visited by more than 32,000 people. A smattering of international opponents to the Council's pro-privatization agenda assembled in the cold, draughty halls of the old buildings where the forum was held and launched the Blue Planet Project as a countervailing force. We were a global network of water justice activists, whose coordinating office was soon to be housed in Ottawa. We were not part of the formal program, but we interrupted many of the sessions chaired by the World Bank and the big water corporations and got a lot of media attention with our opposing vision. It was my first big personal confrontation with the "lords of water," as I called them, but it would not be my last.

The 3rd World Water Forum was held three years later in Kyoto, Japan. By this time, our movement had started to coalesce, and our presence at the forum was markedly different. The Blue Planet Project, Public Services International and other anti-privatization groups were formally invited to participate and given prestigious platforms from which to speak. I was invited to visit Japan ahead of time to meet with one of the key organizers of the forum and brought him and his wife one of my mother's lovely sumi-e watercolour paintings — a red robin on a bare tree branch covered with snow. I was also invited to co-chair an important platform on water governance. It was clear that the powers in the World Water Council still hoped they could bring us into the tent. It soon became apparent that they could not. We used the occasion to challenge the official vision statement of the World Water Council, which promoted public-private partnerships, and released our own alternative vision statement, energizing Japan's fledgling people's water justice movement.

By the time the 4th World Water Forum was held in March 2006 in Mexico City, we were strong enough in organization and numbers to hold our own parallel event. We launched the International Forum in the Defence of Water with 35,000 people marching through the streets of Mexico City. More than 1,000 activists, peasants, academics and government officials attended our gathering that ended with a rally and concert at the famous plaza, Zócalo, where I gave a speech on the right to water to 20,000 people. The first and last time I felt like a rock star!

With each of these forums, our influence grew and our movement became more organized. Pushbacks against water privatization were taking place in many countries; around the world, a grassroots movement was building. At the time of the inaugural World Water Forum in 1997, in fact, the first "water war" was taking place in Cochabamba, Bolivia.

There the people had risen up against Bechtel, the private water company that the government had contracted with in exchange for World Bank funding. Not only did the company raise the price of water out of the reach of this mainly Indigenous population, it had also claimed to own the rain coming from the sky and penalized anyone found capturing rainwater. The people formed the Coalition in Defence of Water and Life, one of the first resistance groups to water privatization in the world. The government sent in the army to quell the ensuing street demonstrations. Protesters were beaten and one young man was killed, but the people kicked the company out of their city and then did the same with Suez, the private water company running the water services in the capital city of La Paz.

I visited Bolivia several times in the aftermath of that struggle and asked Oscar Olivera, a shoemaker by trade and one of the leaders of the resistance, where he got the courage to stand up to an army for water. He simply replied, "Because I would rather die of a bullet than thirst."

Similar resistance efforts were taking place across Latin America, one of the early frontlines of the water wars. In 1992, the government of Mexico had passed a law promoting the privatization of the country's water services; within a decade, many municipalities' services were being run by foreign water companies. This led to the formation of the Coalition of Mexican Organizations for the Right to Water. A similar organization in Ecuador, the Coalition for the Defence of Water, forced the mayor of Quito, the capital, to back down from a planned privatization scheme. Seven thousand citizens of Buenos Aires,

Argentina, attended a conference in November 2002 to protest the massive dumping of contaminated water into the Río de la Plata by the Suez subsidiary that had run the city's water systems for almost a decade.

An important milestone was marked the following year: in August 2003, a coalition of grassroots networks of the Americas called Red VIDA — the Inter-American Vigilance for the Defence and the Right to Water — was formed. It was clear to all of us active in the water justice movement that the more groups and communities that worked together, the stronger we would be. The founding statement of the coalition referred to water as a "public good and an inalienable human right to be protected and promoted by all who inhabit the planet."

Marcela Olivera is a founding member of Red VIDA, the Latin American coordinator for Food & Water Watch and Oscar's younger sister. She says that she cannot imagine the victories they have won across Latin America without this network. She believes that meeting in person and setting up relationships built on trust and respect has been crucial in the fight against water privatization. Though she recognizes there have been huge successes in maintaining water in public hands, she adds that to resist privatization is not enough. "We have to be capable of imagining and creating alternatives," Marcela wrote in an email to me. "We still have some ways to go to make sure that we, the people, are not left behind when it is about participating in the decisions relating to water."

Resistance and water wars were not solely happening in Latin America. The government of India had adopted a

National Water Policy in 2002 that called for private water services wherever feasible. This opened the floodgates to the water barons but it also led to fierce citizen pushback. Mumbai was one of the first Indian cities to begin the process of privatizing its water services and, under the guidance of the World Bank, put together a consortium of foreign water operators to bid on the contract. City officials, however, soon came up against a coalition of social activists, academics and citizens who formed Mumbai Pani — Mumbai Water — to mount a strong opposition to the project, including large demonstrations in which some were arrested. In 2007, the Mumbai municipal government retreated from its privatization plan and confirmed its commitment to public management of the city's water supply.

The water services in Manila, Philippines, were contracted out to a foreign water company in 1997, as were the water services in Jakarta, Indonesia, in 1998. In both cases, this led to fierce domestic resistance movements. In December 2003, an Asia-Pacific network to protect the right to water was launched in Bangkok by Jubilee South and several other justice organizations. In 2007, the South African Coalition Against Water Privatization was formed to fight the decision to bring Suez in to run the water system of Johannesburg. Wherever water privatization spread, so too did resistance to it.

We met regularly at the World Social Forum (WSF), an annual gathering of activists, environmentalists, academics, Indigenous Peoples and other progressives organized as a counterpoint to the elite gathering of the World Economic Forum held in Davos, Switzerland. The first was held in January 2001 in Porto Alegre, Brazil, chosen partly because the city has a strong citizen governance movement and partly because it boasted a great public water system. The WSF is held in a different city every year, and on its return to Porto Alegre in 2005, an astonishing 150,000 people attended from all over the world.

By the time of the next World Water Forum in 2009, we had also held large gatherings in Vancouver, Johannesburg, Delhi, Nairobi and Paris. Our forum had produced a significant body of international research, books, reports, documentaries and testimonials on fighting water commodification. Our movement was supported by public sector unions, such as COSATU in South Africa and the Canadian Union of Public Employees in Canada. Public Services International, the international coalition of public service unions, became an important partner. They worked with us in the global water justice movement, including on the Blue Planet Project, on campaigns to protect public water and public sector water workers and on funding and publishing detailed research, which the movement uses to anchor our arguments.

With all that had taken place, it was little surprise to us that the 2009 World Water Forum held in Istanbul, Turkey, was more hostile to our presence. The WWF had also grown over the decade, and this one had more than 30,000 participants from more than 182 countries. For the first time, there was a heads-of-state meeting to produce and promote a "ministerial statement," and security was particularly tight. Turkey had put out an open call to foreign investors to provide the capital for an extensive series of dams proposed or underway in the country and for water privatization services. Even before the conference began, police attacked peaceful anti-dam protesters outside the venue with dogs, rubber bullets and water cannons. Non-Turkish protesters were deported.

We did hold our own meetings, but the political culture in Turkey made the scene more fraught than it had been in Mexico City or Kyoto. We managed to secure one of the few venues inside the forum set aside for opposing voices, and there I read a statement from Father Miguel d'Escoto Brockmann, then president of the United Nations General Assembly. In it, he voiced his opposition to the pro-corporate nature of the World Water Forum and called on the World Bank and the big water companies to turn the forum over to the UN for all future gatherings. I felt targeted on several occasions that week and was even body-checked by a female official as I stood in a doorway watching the limos pull up at the VIP entrance where elite invitees were being whisked away to a private lounge.

The battle was heating up.

Fighting for the right to water

As we worked to oppose water commodification around the world, we realized that the human right to water and sanitation had to be formalized and recognized at the United Nations. Water had not been included in the 1948 Universal Declaration of Human Rights because, at that time, water was not perceived to have a human rights dimension and was also felt to be virtually limitless. A half century later, as the struggle over water intensified, the fact that water was not a recognized human right — akin to the right to free speech, the right of assembly and the right not to be tortured — meant that political decisions around access to water gravitated toward those institutions that had the power to take advantage of water commodification.

Lobbying for a UN resolution on the right to water had started in the 1990s with partial success, most notably the 2002 adoption by the UN Committee on Economic, Social and Cultural Rights of what was called General Comment No 15. It recognized that the right to water was a prerequisite for realizing other already recognized rights and that water is "indispensable for leading a life in dignity." While this was welcomed as a step forward, we in the movement insisted that a General Comment was to be viewed as an interpretation of another convention or treaty but was not in itself a treaty or convention. In 2004, several organizations, including Germany's Bread for the World, the Right to Water program at the UN Centre on Housing Rights and Evictions, the European office of Food & Water Watch and the Canada-based Blue Planet Project, came together to form Friends of the Right to Water and to enlist the support of movements around the world.

Meanwhile, a number of countries introduced their own laws to protect the right to water. In 1998, South Africa passed the National Water Act, replacing the previous water law of 1956 that was not only openly racist in how water was allocated but was also inappropriate for a water-stressed country. Hailed as revolutionary, the act declared that the water of South Africa is a natural resource that belongs to all the people and that it must be used beneficially and in the public interest. It guaranteed a certain amount of free water to every household and incorporated the principle of subsidiarity, whereby the management of water rests at the most local appropriate level. The fact that water injustice still plagues South Africa is a long and complicated story tied to its history of apartheid and the poverty and racial discrimination that persists today. Nevertheless, this law was an important win for the water justice movement in South Africa and formed a basis for future action.

Across the Atlantic Ocean, Uruguay made history when, on October 31, 2004, it became the first country in the world to recognize the human right to water. Friends of the Earth Uruguay and the anti-water privatization group National Commission for the Defence of Water and Life collected more than 300,000 signatures on a plebiscite — which they delivered to their parliament as a "human river" — for a referendum they overwhelmingly won. I travelled to Uruguay twice during this incredible campaign and can attest to the commitment and sacrifice so many made to fulfill this dream. The legislation itself is still groundbreaking: not only is water considered a human right in Uruguay but social considerations must take precedence over economic ones when the government forms water policy.

Others followed suit: Kenya, Bolivia, Ecuador, Ethiopia,

France, Belgium and the Netherlands all voted to include references in their constitutions or adapted their water laws to recognize the right to water. The United Nations launched its Millennium Development Goals in 2000, vowing to eradicate poverty and hunger and to halve the number of people with no access to safe drinking water and sanitation by 2015. Pressure was building inside the UN to do more.

In 2008–2009, the UN General Assembly chose Father Miguel d'Escoto Brockmann as president and he invited me to volunteer as his senior advisor on water. Together with Pablo Solón, Bolivia's ambassador to the UN, we set out to put a resolution before the General Assembly. We were up against formidable enemies. The World Bank and the World Water Council continued to refuse to recognize the human right to water, calling it a "need" instead. The big water utilities and bottled water companies backed by big food corporations openly opposed us. Then Nestlé CEO Peter Brabeck-Letmathe famously quipped that the notion of the human right to water was "extreme," for which he was widely criticized. Great Britain, the United States, Australia and Canada all opposed the resolution, not wanting to be held accountable for violations taking place in their own countries.

Undeterred by the opposition and refusing to compromise on the language of the resolution, Ambassador Solón challenged the General Assembly on July 28, 2010, to recognize the human right to water and sanitation as "essential for the full enjoyment of the right to life." The resolution also called on member states and international organizations to assist developing countries that would have difficulty in fulfilling their new responsibility to deliver safe, clean drinking water and sanitation to their people. The vote was overwhelming: 122 countries voted in favour and 41 abstained. No country actually voted nay.

Two months later, the UN Human Rights Council spelled out the obligations under the resolution and clarified that it is binding on governments and they must provide regular progress reports to the UN. It also clarified that governments have the primary responsibility to deliver these new rights. In a surprise about-face, the United States, a new member of the Human Rights Council, declared it was "proud" to support the resolution.

It was only a matter of time before the right to water and sanitation was universally adopted. Every UN member state signed *The Future We Want*, the outcome document of the 2012 United Nations Conference on Sustainable Development, which reaffirmed the human right to water and sanitation. And in December 2013, the UN General Assembly tabled a resolution affirming the human right to water and sanitation again. This time, the vote was unanimous. In 2015, the General Assembly recognized water and sanitation as two distinct rights in yet another unanimously adopted resolution.

However, during the negotiations for a new set of UN Sustainable Development Goals (SDGs) to replace the first set due to expire in 2015, it became clear that the fight was not over. The UN is not a monolithic institution and does not generally speak with one voice. It is also a contested arena for economic and foreign policies, with some favouring public control of essential services and some — both national governments and UN officials — promoting privatization. While the General Assembly had voted in favour of the human right to water, not everyone was happy with this and other interests were still at work to walk back this commitment.

The private sector had become quite involved in the implementation of the post-2015 development agenda, and powerful corporations gained privileged access to the process through "multi-stakeholder partnerships." They attempted to exclude the rights language in SDG number 6, the one dealing with water, and to focus simply on improving "access to water" and "water efficiency." The Blue Planet Project and the NGO Mining Working Group fought hard to have the language of human rights included in the new water goals. Their hard work paid off: on August 2, 2015, UN member states unanimously pledged to ensure universal access to safe and affordable drinking water for all by 2030 and agreed to "reaffirm our commitments regarding the human right to safe drinking water and sanitation."

Implementing the right to water

Under the human right to water and sanitation, governments have three obligations:

1. the Obligation to Fulfill, meaning they must come up with a plan and timetable to deliver clean water and sanitation services to their people;

2. the Obligation to Respect, which means that governments must refrain from any action or policy, such as water cut-offs, that interferes with this right; and

3. the Obligation to Protect, which means that governments are obliged to prevent third parties, such as mining companies or factory farms, from polluting the water sources needed by communities.

Countries are moving to meet these obligations in a variety of ways. In early 2012, Mexico amended its constitution to recognize the right to water and sanitation. Three years later, the government was forced to back down after introducing a water bill that would have privatized Mexico's water. A strong grassroots opposition successfully argued that privatization would violate the constitutional amendment the government had so recently adopted. Anti-fracking groups in Mexico are also citing the constitutional recognition of the right to water in their fight to protect the country's groundwater.

In 2014 in Delhi, the municipal AAP party campaigned on the lack of access to clean water and the recognition of the UN resolution on the human right to water. In 2015, after having gained power, the new city government made good on its promise of providing 20,000 litres of free water per month to every household. Commercial and industrial users were not included in the commitment and still paid water rates.

To meet its UN obligation, the government of Rwanda

pledged to provide its entire population with water and sanitation services by 2020. WaterAid reports that almost three in five Rwandans now have a decent toilet and clean water, a major undertaking in a country that so recently emerged from a brutal civil war.

Tanzania has had a water crisis for decades. Nearly half the population of 52 million people has no access to clean drinking water or sanitation, and many die every day from contaminated surface and groundwater. Even though Tanzania has one of the fastest growing economies in Africa, inequality is entrenched, and it has proven hard to improve these numbers. In 2003, the country came under pressure from the World Bank to privatize its water services and contracted the British utility Biwater to operate the services. Over the next four years, the crisis only got worse and more people died. In 2017, the government took Biwater to court in London for breach of contract and won, receiving US\$7 million in damages.

There is renewed hope today in Tanzania. The government has set a goal of access to water for all by 2020. Aid agencies WaterAid, Water.org and the Water Project, along with the Canadian government, are helping to transform the role of women and girls in the fight for water for all. As reported by the CBC in November 2018, women who were water carriers are now becoming engineers, teaching other women and girls how to install and maintain water towers in their villages. The installation of a water tower in the village of Kakora, alongside an education project on hygiene, has greatly reduced the cases of waterborne illnesses. Cholera is down 90% in less than a year. And, reports the CBC, girls are returning to class, freed from the need to fetch water daily and secure in the knowledge that there are safe toilets for them to use at school.

Activists and many government officials in Slovenia are worried about the influx of foreign food and bottled water companies that have bought up significant local water resources. They are also concerned about how these companies could use free trade agreements, such as the Canada-EU Comprehensive Economic and Trade Agreement (CETA), to claim this water as their own or seek compensation if they were denied access. A citizens' initiative collected more than 51,000 signatures to propose a constitutional amendment to protect their water sources and keep them under public control. In response, in November 2016, the National Assembly of Slovenia passed an amendment to its constitution recognizing the human right to water and affirming that water resources are a public good, not a commodity, and as such must be managed by the state, and that drinking water must be supplied by the public sector on a not-for-profit basis.

Activists in various countries are using their domestic courts to promote the rights to water and sanitation. And nation-states are now required to ensure that their laws are interpreted consistently with their human rights obligations, explains WaterLex, a network of legal experts working within the UN. In their 2014 report, *The Human Rights to Water and Sanitation in Courts Worldwide*, the group says that the courts add another protective layer to ensure that these rights are enforced in practice, not just as a statement on paper.

A 2013 French law that banned water cut-offs was challenged in court by the giant water utility Saur, but the French court upheld the law in March 2015, saying that it is unconstitutional to cut off water to anyone for reasons of inability to afford the rates. That same year, a judge in Flint, Michigan, issued an order prohibiting the city from shutting off water services to people for non-payment and required the city to reduce water rates significantly. In December 2016, the Bombay High Court ruled that that city's civic government was duty bound to supply water to illegal slums as people have the right to water under India's constitution. The Kalahari Bushmen of Botswana used the 2010 UN resolution to regain access to their water bore-holes that the government had smashed in an attempt to move them off their traditional homeland.

In March 2015, weeks after the Indonesian constitutional court deemed a World Bank–imposed water law to be anti-constitutional for allowing the privatization of water, the Central Jakarta District Court annulled a 17-year-old public-private partnership, arguing that it violated the human right to water. A year later, the Jakarta High Court overturned this ruling, leading the citizen-led Coalition of Jakarta Residents Opposing Water Privatization to take the matter to the Supreme Court of Indonesia. In April 2017, the supreme court noted that the management of water systems "must be in accord with the United Nations principles and values of human rights" and terminated the policy of water privatization in Jakarta, restoring public management of the city's drinking water. A second supreme court ruling launched by the Ministry of Finance in early 2018 appeared to contradict this first one, leading to great confusion. But under the advice of an expert committee including Nila Ardhianie with the Amrita Institute for Water Literacy, the Jakarta governor announced in February 2019 that he would abide by the first ruling and terminate the private water contracts.

These are important victories. But they must always be vigilantly monitored. As Reza Sahib with the Indonesian grassroots group KRuHA explains, the trap of private contracts already signed is deep and complicated and there is no simple way out without risk. There will always be a need for the grassroots to bridge political debates into everyday reality, he says.

It is also essential to link the human right to water and sanitation with the need to maintain water as a public trust. As we discussed in chapter one, Chile has arguably the most commodified water on Earth. Following the Pinochet-era policy that allowed the massive privatization of the country's water sources — a water market that has benefitted large agribusiness and transnational mining companies — successive Chilean governments extended the private water model to water services. Within a decade, all of the country's municipal water services had been contracted out to large private utilities, many of them foreign. The companies were allowed to charge consumers the full cost of their investments, including the returns to their shareholders. As a result, Chilean water rates became among the highest in Latin America.

But change would come. In November 2016, under pressure from communities and activists across the country, the government of then president Michelle Bachelet approved a new bill for water reform that replaced the Pinochet water law. The new law confirmed water as a human right, prioritized water for human consumption and sanitation as well as ecosystem conservation, guaranteed the rights of Indigenous Peoples and ended the practice of perpetual water rights, converting them to concessions.

However, the private companies running the water services have resisted reform and they still hold a lot of control. They have hung on to their water contracts, and it has been difficult to implement true change to date. Chile is one of the most water-stressed countries in the world, and it is at risk of serious scarcity from climate change. The World Resources Institute says that water availability in Chile's capital Santiago is predicted to fall by 40% by 2070. A May 2016 MIT study called *Equity Impacts of Urban Land Use Planning for Climate Adaptation* looked at cities around the world and found that private influence over water services leaves poor communities more vulnerable to climate change. When water is treated as a commodity, it is more likely to be allotted to projects that make a profit and to wealthy urban areas, displacing the poor and vulnerable to even more precarious living conditions. Unless Chile moves to take back its water under public management, it will be very difficult to deliver on the promise of the human right to water for all.

In El Salvador, Latin America's most water-scarce country, 98% of the water is contaminated. In 2012, El

Salvador adopted a constitutional amendment recognizing the human right to water after a passionate campaign led by Foro del Agua, a water justice coalition of more than 100 organizations. And in 2016, the country adopted a General Water Law that would define and protect water as a human right, ensure its universal access and establish a hierarchy of access to water governed by state institutions, not corporations. But once the right wing party ARENA took power in 2018, it invited the private water sector to sit on the regulatory oversight committees of a new Comprehensive Water Law, and the people have once again had to take to the streets to fight what they see as the back-door privatization of their water. Hundreds protested outside congress on March 20, 2019, vowing to take to the streets until the promise of a constitutional amendment to ensure the human right to water is fulfilled. They cited a study by the national ombud's office that without action, water shortages will make life in El Salvador impossible by the end of the century.

Despite the progressive language of South Africa's 1998 water law, water-conservation measures introduced by the government of Cape Town in early 2018 to deal with the area's multi-year drought had deeply uneven social impacts. As Meera Karunananthan of the Blue Planet Project notes in a July 2018 report for Public Services International, vast inequities already existed in the post-apartheid city where 25% of the population does not have access to piped water at home. Yet Coca-Cola gets to take 530 million litres of municipal water per year at its local plant. Setting targets for water reduction that don't account for the deeply unjust system of water distribution can only make life harder for those already marginalized. For the human right to water to be truly realized, we must challenge the underlying and historical power dynamics that produce social and economic injustice in the first place.

Nevertheless, the nations of the world, on behalf of their people, have now clearly stated that water and sanitation are fundamental human rights. This is a milestone victory for the global water justice movement and for the untold millions struggling for clean water every day. And it has had results. Almost four dozen countries have now either enshrined the right to water within their national constitutions or have framed the right within national legislation. The 2019 United Nations World Water Development Report *Leaving No One Behind* says that between 2000 and 2015, global basic drinking water service increased from 81% to 89%. Now, 181 countries have achieved an average of over 75% coverage for at least basic drinking water services and 154 have achieved over 75% coverage for basic sanitation services.

Armed with the UN resolutions, our movement found new energy to fight the commodification of water and its proponents. In a water justice alliance "Civil Society Statement" released to coincide with the 6th World Water Forum held in Marseilles, France, in March 2012, we laid down a challenge: the five forums held by the World Water Council over nearly two decades had not brought the planet any closer to a solution to the water crisis. Instead, the forum had promoted strategies for corporations to gain greater profits. The recognition of water and sanitation as human rights, we said, moved the stakes back to where they belonged — with governments. It was time, we said, for the United Nations and its member states to take the lead in ensuring progressive implementation of these rights.

At the 7th World Water Forum held in Daegu, Korea, in March 2015, we stood in solidarity with the local water workers union in their fight to stop the privatization of the country's water. And at the 8th World Water Forum held in Brasilia in March 2018, thousands marched to sound the alarm over massive new dams, fracking exploration and threats to the Guarani Aquifer.

We are still fighting every day to move this agenda forward. We win some; we lose some. But slowly awareness is building, and change is happening.

Local resistance grows

There are many campaigns against bottled water companies around the world. In chapter one, I wrote about Coca-Cola bottled water operations in India forced to close by local communities or courts. The company arrived in India in 1999 and set up dozens of pumping and bottling operations using already rapidly depleting groundwater sources. The India Resource Centre, a group that works with communities in India to resist water commodification, reports that by 2016 Coca-Cola has been forced to shutter five of its 24 plants. The company is also under a court-ordered investigation into several of its other plants for illegally

discharging untreated effluents. The water takings of both
Coca-Cola and PepsiCo have garnered a lot of national
media attention, as has the plight of villagers and farmers
left with polluted lands and depleted water supplies. It has
been the affected local communities and grassroots activists, supported by the international movement, that can
take credit for these closings. Local activism works.

In its February 2018 report *Take Back the Tap: The Big
Business Hustle of Bottled Water,* Food & Water Watch tells
of the alarming increase in both bottled water production
in the U.S., but it also notes local campaigns to drive the
companies out. According to the report, sales of bottled
water now exceed those of soft drinks, and 70% of used
plastic water bottles in the U.S. are not recycled. It also
reveals that a stunning two-thirds of bottled water in
the U.S. actually comes from municipal tap water. But
of course, one pays a premium for the bottled version of
the very water that we already can get safely in our own
homes for pennies. Nestlé continued to pump California
groundwater during the state's most recent drought. Its
California water use increased by 19% in the years between
2011 and 2014, the height of the drought, and the company
drew particular criticism during these years for pumping
water on a permit that had been expired for nearly three
decades in the San Bernardino National Forest.

Food & Water Watch launched its Take Back the
Tap campaign on university campuses several years ago;
Corporate Accountability International has a similar
campaign called Think Outside the Bottle. Today, more
than 70 colleges and universities in the U.S. have passed full

or partial bottled water bans, and many more have increased access to public tap water by installing on-campus water fountains and bottle filling stations. A similar campaign in Canada led by the Canadian Federation of Students, Sierra Youth and the Polaris Institute led to a wave of universities going bottled-water free. The University of Winnipeg was first in 2009 and others soon followed suit, among them McGill in Montreal and York University in Toronto. When the administration at the University of Toronto made the decision to go bottled-water free, the students association put out a statement saying that bottled water turns a basic human right into a commodity and expressed its pride in its school.

Around the world, opposition to the privatization of public services has been growing as part of a back-lash against economic globalization and its false promise of universal benefits. In June 2017, the Transnational Institute and the European Federation of Public Unions published a report called *Reclaiming Public Services*. Re-municipalization is taking place in small towns and capital cities alike, which have grown tired of rising prices, labour conflict and the ever-declining service quality of private for-profit operations, said the authors. They note that since 2000, there have been at least 835 examples in 45 countries where municipalities have brought back under public management energy, water and social services, among others, that had been contracted out to private companies.

One might be forgiven for thinking, says the report, that the future inevitably holds more privatization and more inefficient and expensive services that benefit a few wealthy companies. But their research tells a different story: "In reality, below the radar, thousands of politicians, public officials, workers and unions and social movements are working to reclaim or create effective public services that address the basic needs of people and respond to our social, environmental and climate challenges."

Between 2000 and 2018, 267 municipalities around the world that had privatized their water services brought them back under public management, and many more are in the process of doing the same. The bulk of these — 106 — are in France, the country with the longest history of water privatization. It also happens to be home to the two largest private water utilities, Suez and Veolia. While most of this water re-municipalization activity has so far been concentrated in high-income countries, public water operators from the global North are assisting workers and activists in the South to support the process there.

The United States has also witnessed a large surge in the re-municipalization of water services. In its February 2016 report, *The State of Public Water in the United States*, Food & Water Watch notes that communities across the U.S. are moving away from water privatization and "toward local, public, democratic control of our water," despite the aggressive lobby of the big private water operators. In its ten-year history, the organization has helped stop more than three dozen privatization attempts. And in November 2018, after a vigorous grassroots campaign, Baltimore became the first major U.S. city to ban water privatization altogether by amending the city's charter.

Those fighting water privatization in the U.S. are not oblivious to the practices of international institutions sponsored and funded by its government that promote these politics in poor countries. In a hard-hitting letter to the World Bank in June 2016, U.S. Congresswoman Gwen Moore, who plays a powerful role on the U.S. congressional committee overseeing the bank, condemned its water practices. She called for an immediate end to all funding and promotion of water privatization, linking what was happening in poor communities around the world to the loss of control of the water system in Flint, Michigan, that had led to its terrible health crisis. In her letter, Congresswoman Moore wrote, "Water access is a fundamental human right no matter where you live," adding that the World Bank has a responsibility to put its mission — alleviating global poverty — above the pursuit of profit.

While many of the policies and practices concerning water and water justice are national or international in origin, Moore and others are saying that their impact is always local. Higher levels of government can change life for local communities, people and ecosystems. But what the grassroots water justice movement has taught us is that it is equally true that local action and resistance can impact higher levels of government, even the General Assembly of the United Nations itself. The next step is a positive campaign for change from below promoting these hard-won victories. The stage is now truly set for a blue revolution of Blue Communities.

CHAPTER THREE

Blue Communities
Take Root in Canada

It might seem strange that the Blue Communities project
first originated in Canada, since the country is blessed with
water and the provision of drinking water and sanitation
is mostly a public service. But Canada is not without its
water issues and struggles, and the fight for water justice
has taken deep root in recent years.

It is said that Canada has 20% of the world's freshwater but this is only true if we were to drain every lake
and river in the country. In fact, Canada has about 6.5%

of the planet's accessible water, that is, the water we can use without overextraction. This myth of abundance has made generations of Canadians cavalier about water, and we are seeing the effects of this in our own time.

As I documented in my 2016 book, *Boiling Point: Government Neglect, Corporate Abuse and Canada's Water Crisis*, Canadians have taken their water heritage for granted, polluting it with impunity and leaving it unprotected by law. Lakes in Canada are warming faster than in most other parts of the world. And huge, deep Lake Superior is one of the fastest warming major lakes on the planet. All of our glaciers are melting; scientists warn that Canada will lose 80% of its mountain glaciers within the next 50 years. In the North, permafrost melt swells Arctic lakes at first but, with time, they dry up and disappear. Wetlands and forests — vital to the health of lakes and rivers — are being destroyed at an alarming rate. Canada now leads the world in the destruction of untouched forests.

The growth in factory farms and export-driven agribusiness, with their heavy use of chemicals and fertilizers, has put water in jeopardy from runoff nutrient loading, called eutrophication. Hundreds of lakes in Canada are contaminated with blue-green algae, or cyanobacteria, a neurotoxin dangerous to human and aquatic health. Environmental experts have long criticized Canada's lax standards on pesticides and chemicals and the fact that Canada allows the widespread use of glyphosate, the active ingredient in Monsanto's Roundup Ready herbicide and the hormone disrupter atrazine, to name just two herbicides that harm our waters. The use of chemicals in industrial farming is cited as a major cause of insect decline around the world by a meta-study published in the April 2019 edition of the journal *Biological Conservation*. Calling it "insect Armageddon," the researchers report that more than 40% of insect species are now threatened with extinction.

Canada's water protection laws are completely inadequate. There are no national standards for drinking water, groundwater is largely unregulated and unmapped and there is still too much untreated or semi-treated sewage dumped into our waterways every year.

In just one example, Ontario's former environment watchdog Dianne Saxe published her annual report in late November 2018, saying she couldn't believe how much "filth" the government allowed into the province's lakes and rivers. She reported that in the last year alone, raw sewage had overflowed into Ontario waterways 1,327 times. Mere days after this report, the provincial Conservative government announced the elimination of the office of the Environmental Commissioner of Ontario, 25 years after it had been created, merging the once independent watchdog office with that of the auditor general. This move ended the commission's statutory mandate to publish an annual report on government progress on the environment and to uphold the Environmental Bill of Rights that gave Ontario residents the right to participate in environmental policy and hold the government accountable for its care of the province's land, water and air.

The only real water protection laws Canadians had — the Fisheries Act, the Navigable Waters Protection

Act (renamed the Navigation Protection Act) and the Canadian Environmental Assessment Act — were gutted by the previous Conservative federal government, leaving 99% of all lakes and rivers in Canada unprotected by federal law. Under the current Liberal government, the Fisheries Act has been reinstated and improved. The other gutted laws are being addressed in a current omnibus bill intended to modernize how projects such as pipelines, hydro dams and mines are reviewed. These proposed revisions have met with mixed reviews.

While assessments would now take into consideration climate change, the public interest and the impact on Indigenous Peoples — a positive development — it is unclear just which projects will be subject to review. Green Party leader Elizabeth May warns that tar sands projects could still be exempted from review, and Council of Canadians water campaigner Emma Lui says that the replacement for the Navigation Protection Act still does not protect every lake and river, leaving communities to apply to have their waterways included.

The Liberal government claims to have kept one important promise — to provide clean drinking water to First Nations in Canada, thereby ending a terrible part of Canada's history. According to a December 19, 2018, report by Indigenous and Northern Affairs Canada, there were 105 drinking water advisories in First Nations communities in 2015 when Prime Minister Justin Trudeau promised to provide drinking water to all First Nations with long-term water issues. In early 2018, the Indigenous Services department added 250 First Nations water systems to the list needing repair. This brought the total of drinking water advisories temporarily to 129. By mid-December 2018, however, that number had been reduced to 64 with the prediction that most long-term advisories will end by 2020. In the 2019 budget, the federal government earmarked another $739 million over five years on its promise to eliminate drinking water advisories by 2012. However, Emma Lui warns that the government separated "short-term" drinking water advisories from "long-term," thereby making the numbers look better.

As well, the decision by the Trudeau government to buy the Kinder Morgan pipeline is a broken promise to many First Nations. The Union of British Columbia Indian Chiefs opposes the project. The Kinder Morgan pipeline would carry Alberta bitumen — arguably the dirtiest oil on Earth — over 1,355 waterways, many of them through First Nations territories and parks, to the Pacific Coast tanker terminal.

Fighting Nestlé and water privatization

The origin of the Blue Communities project in Canada started with the battles against bottled water takings and the privatization of municipal water services. While there have been a number of bottled water skirmishes across the country, the biggest one to date has been the fierce opposition to Nestlé and its operations in the Guelph area of Ontario.

Nestlé pumps up to 4.7 million litres per day from two wells in this area, despite the fact that its permits to do so have expired. Until recently, the company was paying only $3.71 per million litres — pure theft of a public water supply. In 2016, the company bought a third well — the Middlebrook Water Company's well — though the township of Centre Wellington was trying to buy it to secure access to drinking water for its growing population. The outcry caused the Ontario government to place a moratorium on this well while a review is held and to raise the cost of the water to $503.71 per million litres. While that may sound like a lot more to pay for this water, it is less than one-twentieth of a penny for a litre of water, which Nestlé then sells for as much as $2.

Six Nations of the Grand River is downstream from these operations and this Indigenous community is demanding that the Nestlé operation be completely shut down. Ninety percent of the community do not have running water in their homes. Their officials point out that this travesty is made worse by the fact that Nestlé is pumping water from wells that sit on a tract of land ceded to them in treaties long ago. At a protest at the Nestlé site in Aberfoyle in late November 2018, Six Nations youth advocate Makasa Looking Horse told the *Guelph Mercury* that it was important to speak out because "Nestlé is stealing the aquifer underneath us, taking water without our permission."

The Council of Canadians released a poll in December 2018 that clearly shows that 82% of Ontario residents want the provincial government to stop issuing permits permanently for extracting groundwater to sell as bottled water, no matter what price the companies are paying for it.

By the spring of 2019, more than 80,000 Canadians had signed the Council's pledge to boycott Nestlé.

Hopes that federal government support for the bottled water industry would lessen under the Trudeau government were dashed when, in February 2017, an Agriculture and Agri-Food Canada report promoted the sale of bottled Canadian water to China. The department lamented the "gap" in sales to China, predicting a huge increase in demand for bottled water in that country as its own water is depleted and contaminated. As much as 80% of China's surface and groundwater is polluted. The report spoke glowingly about the "significant opportunities" for the Canadian industry to expand into China. This water would be pumped from Canadian aquifers, bottled and then leave the country forever, adding to the virtual water export issue mentioned earlier.

Indeed, the tap has already been turned on. Online journal *Water Canada* reported in March 2015 that Chinese business owners are looking to spend millions on Canadian water sources. One is already exporting 200 container loads of mineral water from a well near Chilliwack he bought for $17 million. A year later, Whistler Water Inc., a "leading manufacturer and supplier of premium glacial water" signed a "substantial" investment agreement to promote and market its water in China, according to its press release. The business relationship between the Canadian company and Zhen Partners, a prominent Chinese investment fund, was officially launched in Shanghai on September 1, 2016, at a signing ceremony attended by Prime Minster Trudeau and Chrystia Freeland, then minister of international trade.

As former Council of Canadians political director Brent Patterson pointed out in an April 2017 blog, now that bottled water exports to China have begun, they could be difficult to stop under the investment protection provision of the Foreign Investment Promotion and Protection Agreement (FIPA), which gives Chinese investors the right to sue Canada if it tries to curb or even control the export of its water.

As well as fighting bottled water withdrawals, activists in Canada have been opposing the privatization of water services. The great majority of municipal water services in Canada are publicly managed and delivered as a public service. However, the trend of municipalities looking to save money by contracting out their water services to private water utilities has not bypassed this country.

In 1994, Hamilton, Ontario, leased it water services to a private company only to reverse this decision a decade later as officials became fed up with environmental damage and mismanagement. The private utility they contracted with had been sold four times in that decade. In 1998, Moncton, New Brunswick, signed a controversial 20-year P3 contract with the private water company Veolia for its water filtration facility. In spite of strong public opposition over rising water rates, in a May 2019 closed-door meeting city council extended the contract for another five years. Public resistance forced the city council of Vancouver, British Columbia, to retreat from its 2001 decision to privatize the operation of its filtration plant. In 2011, the citizens of Abbotsford, BC, voted overwhelmingly to reject a proposal by their city council for a

public-private partnership for an infrastructure expansion, and in 2015, the city of White Rock, BC, brought its water services back into public hands.

A number of other municipalities were persuaded to adopt P3s when the former Conservative government brought in a policy that linked federal funding support and privatization. Under its new crown corporation called Public-Private Partnership Canada (PPP Canada), the government introduced new rules whereby any municipality seeking federal funding for upgrading or building new water services infrastructure of more than $100 million must adopt a P3 as a condition. No privatization, no money.

Lac La Biche and Kananaskis, both Albertan towns, were the first to receive federal funding to upgrade their systems through P3s. Saint John, New Brunswick, got $115 million — half from the federal government — in 2013 to contract out its water treatment system. That same year, after a passionate public debate, the city council in Regina, Saskatchewan, voted to contract out its wastewater treatment service after having spent $400,000 promoting the P3 model. Portage la Prairie, Manitoba, decided in 2016 to upgrade its treatment facility through a P3 in exchange for federal funding. And heavy federal funding helped the city of Victoria, BC, to contract out its $765-million wastewater treatment project to a private consortium in 2017.

That year, the Liberal government replaced the PPP Canada crown corporation with the Canada Infrastructure Bank, a $35-billion entity with a similar function but with

a much larger budget and mandate. The conditionality rule linking federal funding for water services to P3s has been cancelled, but the bank still promotes the model.

Many Canadians are concerned about the state of our aging water pipes and treatment plants, as water infrastructure funding across the country has been seriously neglected for decades. In 2016, the Federation of Canadian Municipalities reported that about 40% of wastewater pumping stations and storage tanks in Canada are in various degrees of decline; the estimated cost to replace them is about $61 billion. This figure does not include the funds needed for new water infrastructure in many of Canada's burgeoning cities. The federal government has promised that it would address this issue through the Canada Infrastructure Bank.

The Canadian Union of Public Employees (CUPE) represents public water workers across the country and is acutely aware of the need for investment in Canada's water service systems. While CUPE supports the idea of an infrastructure fund to address the crisis, the union opposes the bank's use of private financing to turn public services into revenue-making projects. They believe this will drive up costs for municipalities, lead to new or increased user fees and tolls and shift planning, ownership and control of public water facilities to for-profit corporations. Governments can borrow at interest rates of less than 2.5% for ten years or more, but private investors will pay closer to 9%, ensuring that water rates will rise to pay the difference.

The first Blue Communities

Concerned about the government promotion of P3s in the fall of 2009, the Council of Canadians and CUPE held a Canada-wide gathering called the Blue Summit. Hundreds of workers, environmentalists, Indigenous and community activists came together in Ottawa to discuss the many ways in which water was coming under corporate control. It had become clear that lobbying the federal government on these issues would be fruitless and that promoting grassroots activism and municipal opposition to the commodification of water was crucial if we were to have any influence. We launched the Blue Communities project there to promote public water management and public drinking water. The idea was to get municipalities across the country to adopt resolutions that would make it harder to privatize their water services.

To become a Blue Community, a municipality must:

1. recognize and protect water and sanitation as human rights;
2. protect water as a public trust by promoting publicly financed, owned and operated water and wastewater services; and
3. ban or phase out the sale of bottled water in municipal facilities and at municipal events.

A Blue Community is founded on the understanding that water, along with other essential resources like air and oceans, is a commons, a cultural and natural resource vital to our survival that must be accessible to all members of a community. It is not privately owned. Rather it is a public trust to be shared, carefully managed and enjoyed by all. Recognizing water as a public trust requires governments to protect water for a community's reasonable use and for future generations. As part of the commons, community rights and the public interest take priority over water use for profit. Public and community management of water require transparent rules of access. Many private companies and industries need water for their operations, but they must be subject to government oversight based on democratically agreed-upon priorities for the use of local water sources.

Recently, the practice of water service cut-offs for non-payment of water bills has become a growing problem. So the Blue Community project added a resolution that, in order to fulfill the first principle that recognizes water and sanitation as human rights, a municipality will refrain from shutting off water and wastewater services to households with an inability to pay their bills and make every effort to work with the residents to remediate the debt. This allows cut-offs to those who can afford but choose not to pay their water bills but does not punish those without the means. In Canada, most municipalities have cut-off policies, but they are seldom used. Quebec alone has a strict policy forbidding water service cut-offs.

CUPE's partnership with the Council of Canadians on the Blue Communities project was a natural extension of our commitment to public water as a basic human right. "The thousands of water workers that CUPE represents make communities throughout Canada both safer and healthier for all citizens," said Paul Moist, former president of CUPE. CUPE asserts that public water and wastewater services are vital to our lives and the foundation of safe and healthy communities. But to be able to rise to this level of service, municipalities need reliable public funding to strengthen and expand water and wastewater systems. The precarious nature of privatization is a threat to these services. The Blue Communities project came at a vital time in the struggle to protect public water services as a basic human right in Canada, added Moist, who reminds us that public sector workers are committed to the health of our water and are vital to protecting it.

Eau Secours is a Quebec-based non-profit founded in 1997 to counter a wave of privatization of water services then taking place in Montreal. It is made up of individuals and organizations from many communities. In 2017, the board decided to join the Council of Canadians and the Canadian Union of Public Employees to launch the Blue Communities / Communautés bleues project in Quebec. In November 2018, Eau Secours launched its official campaign to invite municipalities, First Nations communities and educational institutions from Quebec to become Blue Communities. The launch was held in Amqui, a small town at the confluence of two rivers in Bas-Saint-Laurent, where First Nations have gathered for centuries for their traditional summer powwows, and whose Indigenous name means "place of pleasure." Amqui became the first community in Quebec to go Blue.

Alice-Anne Simard is the director of Eau Secours

and is encouraged by the support, interest and volunteer energy this project has unleashed in just a short time. She is confident that the project will spread quickly and widely in Quebec because it supports collective empower-ment and encourages the development of local change agents: "We believe that the Blue Communities project is an excellent response to the many current issues that affect the protection and management of water, such as the pollution of rivers by untreated wastewater discharges, underfunding, the threat of privatization of water services, the demonization of tap water and the increasing consumption of plastic water bottles." Simard is hopeful that this project can have a positive effect on water justice, especially for racialized, poor, Indigenous and marginal-ized communities.

There are now 27 municipalities in Canada that have become Blue Communities. The first was Burnaby, the third largest city in British Columbia, that made its declaration on World Water Day in 2011. Derek Corrigan, then the city's long-serving mayor, was a fierce proponent of public services and proud to be the first municipality in the country to take this step. The story of Burnaby becoming a Blue Community was widely published in the province and led to the Union of British Columbia Municipalities adopting a resolution in support of the Blue Communities project later that year, calling upon the federal government to adequately invest in public water infrastructure. One of the latest — and largest — municipalities to date is Montreal, Quebec, which became a Blue Community on World Water

Day, March 22, 2019. At that ceremony, the University of McGill became the first post-secondary institution in Canada to become a Blue Community, hopefully paving the way for many more. Quebec now boasts the first high school in the world to become a Blue Community as well as the first Blue school board, Commission scholaire de l'île de Montréal.

In each case, local activists initiated the campaign and lobbied their municipal officials, in some cases over and over, until they succeeded. Sometimes they start with a friendly council member or mayor; other times with city officials. Often they have to build a local network of groups and individuals to show that there is indeed a lot of public support for the project. This often entails townhall meetings and debates, as well as getting informational materials out to key groups, such as NGOs, places of worship and environmental organizations. And because it is a publicly debated issue, the campaigns generate a lot of discussion, media attention and education that creates widespread local public awareness. This is a huge bonus in the broader fight for water justice.

Often, local groups that have worked together on other water-related campaigns move on to promote Blue Communities. Such was the case for Tiny Township on the shores of Lake Huron in Simcoe County, Ontario, where local activists had fought a proposed industrial dump called Site 41 for more than two decades. Site 41 was slated to destroy a great path of farmland and sit atop of the Alliston Aquifer, rated by one German lab as the purest water in the world. After an intense campaign, the groups succeeded in stopping the project in 2009. Highly political and well educated on the issues of water governance and water protection, they went on to other environmental issues, including promoting Blue Communities in their area. Tiny's mayor Ray Millar was a leader in the fight against Site 41 and oversaw his township becoming a Blue Community in September 2011.

Not surprisingly, right from the beginning, Nestlé Canada intervened to try to stop a number of cities from becoming Blue Communities. It lobbied councillors and city officials across the country to discourage them. John Challinor, the company's director of corporate affairs, regularly told city officials that the campaign was political, not environmental, and the proposed ban on bottled water was an "overly simplified, factually incorrect, feel good" initiative of a self-interested union. Several cities have backed away from the project under this pressure. A tie vote of Oshawa, Ontario, city council in March 2013 meant that the city did not become a Blue Community, in spite of the fact that its environmental advisory committee had recommended investigating options to reduce its reliance on bottled water. Nestlé and the Canadian Beverage Association both lobbied hard to defeat the resolution.

Activists from the Mid-Island chapter of the Council of Canadians, CUPE and the Vancouver Island Water Watch presented their case to elected officials of Nanaimo, BC, in early 2012. Immediately thereafter, city council was lobbied hard by Nestlé individually and via the media. Nestlé's John Challinor again argued in the local newspaper that the Blue Communities project has nothing to do with the environment and everything to do with politics, devised "to ban the sale of bottled water in municipal facilities under the guise of human rights and infrastructure management."

Local activist June Ross replied that it is indeed a plot — a "citizen's plot to rid ourselves of plastic bottles that are full of toxins, to rid ourselves of individuals paying 1,000 times the cost to drink bottled water (when in fact we have the best water anywhere that comes out of our taps), to rid our environment of the miles of plastic that have accumulated in our oceans and finally to rid ourselves of a corporation that is making huge profits off a resource that belongs to us citizens and does not belong to a corporation." City council referred the matter to staff for a report on the costs of such a move and, after that report came back favourable, the City of Nanaimo became a Blue Community on September 10, 2012. The groups presented councillors with stainless steel bottles with the logo "Proud to Be a Blue Community."

Thunder Bay sits on the western shore of Lake Superior in northwestern Ontario. Its then mayor, Keith Hobbs, was passionate about the health of the Great Lakes and open to the idea of his city becoming a Blue Community. I spoke on the issue at a 2012 Great Lakes Need Great Friends public forum in Thunder Bay where local activists officially launched the campaign. It was clear from the beginning that they had a receptive mayor and city council. Alarmed at this development, Nestlé's Challinor wrote to city council opposing the proposed resolution and to the local paper, the *Chronicle Journal*, denouncing Blue Communities as a "Trojan horse–like conspiracy." Mayor Hobbs refused to meet with him.

Local water justice activist Janice Horgos wrote a powerful rebuttal to the newspaper saying that the only conspiracy she could see was the private water industry's massive public relations campaign to undermine faith in public water in an effort to divert attention from its corporate takeovers. "Located at the headwaters of the world's largest body of freshwater," she wrote, "becoming a Blue Community will confirm Thunder Bay as a leader in the protection of this shared public resource and help make our community and planet more sustainable." On March 22, 2015, World Water Day, Thunder Bay became a proud Blue Community.

In other cities, the fight has been harder and progresses in stages. Water activists in Prince Albert, Saskatchewan, have gone before their city council on World Water Day every year since 2011 to advocate for becoming a Blue Community. In an interview, activists Rick Sawa and Nancy Carswell explained that they would only be given five minutes each year to promote all three principles together, and each time, the motion for the city to become a Blue Community would be shelved. The sticking point was the issue of banning bottled water, with several councillors worried about how they would supply water at public events if they took this step. However, the group of water activists had secured the support of a new young councillor, and on World Water Day, 2017, he made a motion to adopt the first two principles confirming water as a human right and public trust and proposed that the city continue to debate the third principle. The group considered this to be a huge victory and intends to persevere until all three are adopted. They are raising funds to acquire a water trailer for the city to provide water at municipal events. If the city rents out the trailer, that money can be used to install fountains and refill stations in public facilities and ease the concerns of city council.

Owen Sound Water Watchers have similarly come up against that third principle when their Ontario city adopted the first two resolutions but not the third. Liz Zetlin is a community organizer, passionate environmentalist and Owen Sound's first poet laureate. She says she is inspired by "garlic, rivers, limestone, apostrophes and the backs of squirrels." She has worked tirelessly for more than six years to have her city declared a Blue Community. In 2015, she and her fellow activists presented a petition with more than 600 signatures to city council to take this step, but council still balked. City officials did, however, commit to installing water-filling stations in public spaces across the city. Zetlin called this "a great step forward" and Councillor Richard Thomas, who supports the Blue Communities project, predicted at a May 2018 council meeting that it is only a matter of time before the issue comes up again, as there is a wave of concern about plastics in communities all around the Great Lakes.

Council of Canadians water campaigner Emma Lui keeps track of all the pending municipal campaigns and is convinced that there are many more to come. London, Ontario, banned bottled water in 2008 and is a good candidate. Hamilton is another Ontario city concerned about plastic, and it banned bottled water in May 2018. However, part of its waste incineration is run by a private company, so it is not able to become a full Blue Community. Saskatoon, Saskatchewan, has an active group promoting Blue Communities to city council there, but resistance centres on the lack of public water stations in the city, an obstacle the group is convinced can be overcome with time.

The project has created more than its share of heroes and heroines. When she was just eleven years old, Robyn Hamlyn of Kingston, Ontario, watched a film in her grade seven class about my work and declared to her mother that she would dedicate her life to fighting to protect water. She wrote to the mayor of her city, who invited her to present before city council. Kingston had already banned bottled water and its water was in public hands, so all it needed was to adopt a resolution recognizing water as a human right, which it did. Inspired to do more and supported by her mother, Robyn sent letters to 50 mayors across Ontario and she has gone on to meet with the city councils of 31 municipalities. At least six of these — Niagara Falls, St. Catharines, Welland, Ajax, Clarington and Thorold — directly attribute their decisions to become a Blue Community to Robyn.

Robyn told me that in the early years, she used to get very nervous about presenting to adults at council meetings, but she would remind herself that this was about the global water crisis, something that truly mattered — "not some talent show or school project." Her determination saw her through her fear. She remembers with amusement that, at one meeting, she was giving the statistics on the environmental damage of bottled water and watched as a councillor quietly reached for the bottle of water on her desk and put it under her chair. Asked how she felt about Nestlé coming after her, questioning how a child could know anything about such issues, Robyn said, "I couldn't understand why such a large multi-million dollar company would be so threatened by a 13-year-old presenting to councils to try and save our water that they would actually write articles about how I didn't know what I was doing and then come and present to councils against me." She called the personal attacks "scary."

Robyn's mother has this quote on her fridge: "I am only one, but I am one. I cannot do everything, but I can do something. What I can do, I ought to do; and what I ought to do, by the grace of God, I will do." Robyn says she lives by these words.

The concern about the growing use of bottled water has also been taken up by community groups who work alongside municipal programs and Blue Communities to promote tap water. Ottawa-based Evan Pilkington launched the Blue W program to get businesses, public buildings, shops, cafés and restaurants to encourage the use of tap water by displaying a decal in their window indicating they are places where people can refill their reusable water bottles for free. Evan calls his project a "block parent party for water" and says he and his team have a database of 27,000 venues, mostly in Canada but now spreading around the world. He told me that among his major goals are the reduction of the number of single-use plastic water bottles and the recognition of the hard work of public municipal water workers.

A great deal of learning about local water sources and water management takes place when a municipality goes through the process of becoming a Blue Community. Many people cannot name their local water source, they do not know if it is delivered by a public or private utility and they had not thought to ask which is better. But a community cannot go through this process of becoming Blue without a lot of public debate and information sharing; local citizens become much more water literate as a result

What happens when a municipality is rural and not all citizens are served by a central system? How does a community like this go Blue? The municipality of the District of Lunenburg in Nova Scotia became the first Blue Community in Atlantic Canada in 2015, urged to do so by the South Shore chapter of the Council of Canadians. But this community is largely rural and most households and many businesses depend on individual wells that they own. It was important to clarify that the P3 resolution only applies to for-profit corporations, not private well owners. The Blue resolutions can vary when the circumstances warrant a different approach. Well water is private to the landowner; these sources would not fall under corporate, classic P3 management.

Bayfield, another largely rural community, situated on Lake Huron, is unique in that the resolution to become a Blue Community was adopted by the local residents, organizations and businesses, but not the larger municipality itself. From local restaurants, cafés, inns and stores to the city choir, book clubs and the Girl Guides, giving up plastic bottles became a local project of great pride. Local environmental writer and leader Ray Letheren explains that "Blue Bayfield" made available over 2,000 refillable bottles for redistribution and installed multiple water bottle refilling stations throughout the village that have been used more than 25,000 times in two years. The community also has a mobile water tricycle called Blue Betty, available to all public functions for events and festivals.

In early 2015, the St'át'imc at Tsal'alh located in southwestern BC became the first Indigenous community in Canada to go Blue. Former band chief Garry John said of this decision, "This action upholds positions taken by our ancestors and makes sure our children and grandchildren know that we take our responsibility to keep water pure and free in all respects." The First Nation added a demand that the federal government invest $4.7 billion in water and wastewater infrastructure in Indigenous communities and make adequate funding available without the condition of a P3 agreement.

John's partner Shelley McLean runs the hot lunch program at the local school. They used to serve chocolate milk and packaged fruit juice to the children. Now they serve chilled tap water at each meal. "If a boil water advisory comes up, we're prepared to boil water each day for this invaluable initiative," says John, who adds that they have introduced wild game and local berries into the students' diet as well.

But many Indigenous communities in Canada and around the world do not have accessible clean public water sources and, of course, they therefore cannot pledge to do away with bottled water at this time. It is clear that the long-term goal must be available public water for all, a pledge which can be the substitute for the bottled water ban in places where people must still rely on it for their health.

Faith-based groups in Canada and around the world are turning their attention to both the protection of watersheds and the human right to water. On December 10, 2017, Human Rights Day, the Sisters of St. Joseph of Canada became the first group of religious communities to become Blue. In addition to the three principles, the Sisters added a pledge to urge the government to adopt sustainable policies that give particular attention to the rights of marginalized groups, communities and individuals. "Our commitment to regard water as a basic right calls for developing a culture of care and joining our voices to the cry for justice, respect and responsible sharing of water and to work toward universal access to clean water," said the Sisters in a press release.

When institutions other than municipalities go Blue, they bring new opportunities to spread the word. Paul Baines is the coordinator for the Blue Communities program for the Sisters of St. Joseph. He says that their commitment and others, such as the Sisters of Mercy in St. John's, Newfoundland, allow the different houses to work on the issues of concern locally, be it a First Nations community without water, joining a campaign against a quarry or mine or opposing a bottled water operation. While celebrating the "sacredness of water," the Sisters — "a great reach of a network" — are also able to motivate other faith communities about water issues. Their Blue Community logo says "water is the first medicine."

It has been very gratifying to see this project embraced in Canada. While we do not yet have the laws and regulations in place to truly protect Canada's water heritage, Canadians nevertheless raise a fierce defence when water is threatened. Every commercial scheme to sell Canadian water to the United States has been met with strong resistance, and every export pipeline fight has water protection at its core. A proactive Blue Communities campaign in Canada is a positive step toward truly understanding the sacred nature of water and the need for better protections.

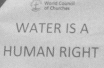

WATER IS A
HUMAN RIGHT

WATER IS A
HUMAN RIGHT

CHAPTER FOUR

Blue Communities Give Hope in Europe

Switzerland first

It never occurred to me to think of this project outside Canada. It was originally conceived as a purely Canadian way of dealing with a federal government intent on privatizing municipal water services at the same time that it was gutting broader water-protection laws.

But in the fall of 2012, I was in Switzerland, where Nestlé is headquartered, taking on the bottled water giant in a number of conference speeches. I was introduced to Alexander Tschäppät, then mayor of Bern, Switzerland's capital; Tschäppät was a social democrat and progressive. I shared my concerns about Nestlé with him and he shared his with me, including the fact that there are no limits in Switzerland to the amount of money corporations can give to politicians and political parties and no rules of disclosure. It is widely understood that Nestlé and other private Swiss corporations give a great deal of money to the political system to maintain the country's business-friendly economic environment.

Not long after I returned home to Canada, I received an invitation to come back: Bern had decided to become the first Blue Community outside Canada. Moreover, the University of Bern and the city's major reform church had also chosen to become Blue Communities. I had never considered the idea of organizations adopting this project, and suddenly the world opened up to endless possibilities.

In a ceremony at Bern's city hall on a sunny September 18, 2013, I proudly presented the certificates to Mayor Tschäppät and University of Bern vice rector Martin Tauber and then to a large congregation of people at the beautiful reform church nearby. These organizations added a fourth principle: to promote public-public partnerships rather than public-private partnerships in the global South. I was so pleased that these institutions had the foresight and courage to take this step and said, "It is my fervent hope that your undertaking today will be the beginning of a European-wide movement that will one day reach across the whole world." In my work, one of the most rewarding things is when far-seeing individuals take an idea and run with it, in this case, pushing the movement into new arenas that I hadn't thought of.

The Swiss Reformed Church took its commitment seriously indeed. Under the guidance of Reverend Heinz Bichsel, head of the ecumenical department serving more than 200 parishes, it established an office to promote the project in Switzerland, and it has spread the concept further than anywhere else. Thanks to the hard work of coordinator Lisa Krebs, there are now 26 Swiss Blue Communities: three cities, 12 churches, six universities, a museum, three workers unions and the NGO HEKS, also known as Swiss Church Aid. All of this in less than a decade.

Franklin Fredrick, originally from Brazil and now living in Switzerland, is a water activist and long-time critic of Nestlé. He recognizes the importance of bringing the Blue Communities project to the country that headquarters the bottled water giant, but he is highly critical of the Swiss government's position on the issue of water commodification internationally. He points out that SDC — the government agency for development and cooperation responsible for the coordination of Swiss international development — not only refuses to oppose public-private partnerships in the developing countries where it operates, but it also refuses to criticize the role Nestlé plays and the profits it makes promoting the privatization of water.

This is not unusual. Many countries whose grassroots movements are successfully fighting the privatization of water domestically support market-based water solutions abroad. This is actually a very powerful argument for building this movement from the bottom up. The stronger the Blue Communities movement becomes, the harder it is for governments to promote water commodification internationally.

Blue Communities spread across Europe

Europe has a long history of public water services, even though the biggest private water utilities are European. However, the financial collapse of 2008 combined with the growing debt of the poorer countries of the EU led to a push to sell off public assets as a condition for debt relief. The European Commission imposed an "austerity" program on countries such as Spain, Italy, Portugal and Greece with water privatization top of the list. Many municipalities began the process of privatizing or partially privatizing their water services in compliance. In response, a movement of public utilities and citizens grew to fight the loss of public water services and they have proven to be unstoppable.

In 2008, Aqua Publica Europea, the European Association of Public Water Operators, was founded to promote the public management of water services and the human right to water. With 65 member public utilities today, the organization has been a steady influence on European water politics and calls on the EU to make public water a priority by guaranteeing safe, accessible and affordable water for all.

In 2012, after the Alternative World Water Forum in Marseilles, a Europe-wide network of activists, unions and researchers founded the European Water Movement. Together with the European Federation of Public Sector Unions, it launched a campaign to revise the European Drinking Water Directive that sets the standards for drinking water protection. The network made use of the European Citizens' Initiative, a new program of the European Commission (EC) meant to increase direct democracy by enabling EU citizens to participate personally in the development of EU policies. If one million citizens from at least one-quarter of the member states sign a petition, the EC is obliged to consider their policy demand.

The water movement's initiative was called Right2Water and listed a set of proposals that would ensure the human right to water and the protection of water as a public trust. With almost two million signatures, the network's project became the first successful European Citizens' Initiative, and the European Commission acknowledged that it was now required to deal with their concerns. As a result, in September 2015, the European Parliament recognized that water is not a commodity but a public good vital to human life and dignity and called for services to be subject to democratic controls.

When the European Commission presented its new Drinking Water Directive to the European Parliament in early 2018, the European Water Movement was encouraged by some parts and disappointed with others. The new rules do improve water safety and encourage the use of tap water over bottled water. They also affirm that water is an essential public service and call on member states to improve access for all their citizens, especially the most vulnerable. As well, they call for an end to the sale of bottled water in EU parliamentary buildings. But the new directive stops short of explicitly recognizing the universal right of access to safe drinking water and sanitation, and does not call for an end to water privatization.

Despite this shortfall in the official directive, the European Economic and Social Committee, an advisory body representing workers' and employers' organizations to the European Parliament, is in favour of adding universal access to water as a principle and has called for a stop to water privatization. As American writer Rebecca Solnit has said, success is not an army marching forward but a crab scuttling sideways: one never knows where or how our allies will appear.

Italy

The same fierce debate is taking place within EC member countries as well. Water privatization in Italy is pervasive. Acea Ato runs the privatized water services in Rome and has been heavily criticized for its rotting infrastructure and water leaks, and there have long been accusations that the Mafia is siphoning off public funds intended for infrastructure upkeep. A shocking 45% of the city's water spills out underground or pools into the street, according to the online labour journal *Revolting Europe*. The climate crisis hit Rome hard in the summer of 2018 when the city's famous water fountains dried up, and the people were forced to live with water shortages and rations. But instead of investing in fixing the problem, the company has paid out 93% of its US$74 million of annual earnings to its shareholders in the years between 2011 and 2015. Outraged by high water tariffs and poor services, it is no surprise that a forceful homegrown opposition arose.

The Forum Italiano dei movimenti per l'acqua, a coalition of trade unions, environmentalists and community activists, was a founding member of the European Water Movement. It held a referendum in June 2011 against a proposed law that would have privatized all of Italy's remaining public water services. Even though 95% of the 27 million Italians who voted opposed the government law, successive governments have continued to promote private water services. This has led to protests and a growing movement at the municipal level of government to protect local water. At a demonstration to oppose water cut-offs in Naples in November 2015, more than 30 mayors, including the mayor of Naples, marched with workers and citizens.

France

The fight against water privatization in France has also created an unexpected coalition of local municipalities and grassroots groups that have taken their water back into public hands. No country in Europe has a deeper history of water privatization. Indeed, the two water giants, Veolia and Suez, got their start running the water systems of hundreds of French villages, towns and cities.

Grenoble was one of the first to privatize in 1989 and the first to change its mind. As documented in a May 2018 report in online journal *openDemocracy*, water rates had soared 56% by 1995 and the city's mayor, Alain Carignon, was indicted for corruption in connection to dealings with the private company. He was found guilty and sent to jail for two years. Under continued public pressure, Grenoble brought its water back under public management in 2001.

Since Grenoble, 105 other towns and cities in France have re-municipalized their water services — more than any other country in the world. This is remarkable since successive French governments have supported Veolia and Suez with subsidies and tax breaks and through the promotion of their business interests internationally.

Paris reclaimed its water from Suez and Veolia in 2010 after 26 years of privatization, ending what the city council called a fragmented, opaque and expensive patchwork of services with poor accountability. The city reintegrated its water services to ensure better oversight and transparency. The public utility Eau de Paris was created to replace the private management structure. Not only has it invested in conservation and the environment, city officials report, it is running the service far more efficiently as it can use all its funds to provide services, rather than keeping back capital to pay shareholders. Within the first year, savings of about 15% were achieved, and water tariffs were lowered by 8% the next year. According to Anne Le Strat, who oversaw the transition as deputy mayor, Eau de Paris has been saving the city council of Paris more than US$40 million per year. Officials at Eau de Paris are enormously proud of their company and promote it and over 1,200 public fountains they have installed in schools and many venues across the city. Their beautiful Pavillon de l'eau is open to the public to learn about the city's water operations and used by the community to promote environmental initiatives and public events.

While there are active water justice organizations such as Attac France and France Libertés, in Paris and right across France, the fight to reclaim the city's water services back under public management and then to designate Paris a Blue Community came largely from within city council. Le Strat's successor, deputy mayor Célia Blauel, is equally committed to public water services. She understands that every victory has to be safeguarded, lest it be lost to complacency. It was an embarrassing and serious blow to the two water companies to lose not only Paris but so many other municipalities in their home country, and they have never stopped trying to get the cities to reconsider their decisions. Blauel and Mayor Anne Hidalgo decided to take the next step to protect their public water company.

On March 22, 2016, World Water Day, I had the great pleasure of presenting the Blue Community certificate to the deputy mayor and other officials at Paris City Hall. Blauel pledged to keep Paris water in public hands for all time. I said, "The global water crisis is getting more serious by the day and is being made worse by the corporate theft and abuse of water. Becoming a Blue Community like Paris has done today is a critical step toward the stewardship of water locally and globally that we need now and for future generations." We spoke again at an evening public forum at the water pavilion attended by a large and enthusiastic crowd. I couldn't miss the two well-dressed men who stood at the back of the room, arms crossed, coolly observing the event. Blauel recognized them as senior officials of Suez and Veolia.

Greece

Greece's two biggest cities, Athens and Thessaloniki, allowed partial privatization of their water companies, EYDAP and EYATH, in the late 1990s; within a short time, the public sector union reported that water rates had risen sharply and services had declined. However, in 2012, the Greek government signed a memorandum with the European Commission, the European Central Bank and the International Monetary Fund, known as the "Troika," that in exchange for debt relief, it would privatize as many public assets as possible, including water services. The government announced that it would contract out the balance of the water systems of Athens and Thessaloniki to the private sector.

In response, the Thessaloniki EYATH union worked with grassroots activists across the city to form a new alliance called Save Greek Water. Its first order of business was to organize a referendum, which was held on May 18, 2014. Ninety-eight percent of the 200,000-plus citizens of the city who voted said no to the privatization of their water. The memorandum directive was stopped in its tracks, and the matter went to the highest administrative court in the country. The Council of State ruled that the sale of Thessaloniki's water services should be exempted from the Troika memorandum. But under continued pressure from Europe, the Greek government signed another memorandum in 2016. All public assets, including water, were put into a superfund to be sold off. In one year, Greece sold 14 regional airports and the ports of Piraeus and Thessaloniki.

Save Greek Water went back to court and back to work, shutting off the water in the offices of government leaders who voted for this development and flooding their inboxes with more than three million messages of protest. (The court case is still pending, at the time of writing.) Dramatically, the network convinced the mayor and city council of Thessaloniki to say no to water privatization and the superfund by becoming a Blue Community on June 4, 2018.

The mayor of Thessaloniki, Yiannis Boutaris, a 76-year-old progressive who has fought right-wing populist movements in his country for many years, was badly beaten the week before the celebration. He had been attending an outdoor human rights ceremony when he was attacked by thugs. I was in Thessaloniki to induct the city as a Blue Community, and Boutaris told me then that he was deeply worried about the rise of the right and its use of violence in his country and across Europe. I was struck by his courage and his words. They reminded me how fragile democracy and human rights really are — and how the fight for them never ends.

Yiorgos Archontopoulos, a leading activist and spokesperson for the EYATH union, knows the future is uncertain. Just because the mayor and city council of one city voted to become a Blue Community does not mean the federal government will cease its plans. But it is a spanner in their works and an important way for the grassroots to assert their rights. Yiorgos is proud that EYATH is an official Blue Ambassador, able to promote Blue Communities in his country on behalf of the Blue Planet project. But he also recognizes that the union couldn't have launched such a powerful opposition to the privatization plans if it had not partnered with civil society organizations and local communities. "Creating Save Greek Water was the most important thing in this struggle," he wrote to me. "It opened the struggle to people that had never ever before involved themselves in movements and turned a union struggle into a city struggle that made history."

Spain

Private water services made deep inroads into Spain in the 1980s, resulting in an even split between private and public control of the country's water utilities. The majority of the private concessions are controlled by Agbar, a subsidiary of Suez, and Aqualia, which has links to Veolia. Water cut-offs in Spain have been common in the years since the financial crisis of 2008. Under pressure from the Troika, Madrid and Barcelona committed to privatizing their water services. In 2012, Agbar was granted a 35-year concession by the city of Barcelona for both its drinking and waste water services to be run as a public-private partnership. The contract was granted without a public tender. Madrid city council prepared to privatize 49% of its water utility, Canal de Isabel II, as well.

But the municipal governments underestimated the opposition they would encounter. AEOPAS, the Spanish association of public water operators, and a newly formed water justice group called Aigua és Vida — *water is life* — launched a national campaign against water privatization. In 2011, as both cities geared up for the handover, water activists in Madrid gathered more than 35,000 names on a petition to stop the privatization of their water and, a year later, organized a referendum on the subject, setting up more than 350 voting booths around the city. An astonishing 166,000 people participated, 165,000 of whom voted to keep their water public. In Barcelona, groups challenged the contract the city had signed, declaring it invalid and taking the case to the Court of Justice in Catalonia.

In 2015, progressive municipal councils were elected in Madrid and Barcelona. Both councils had ties to the progressive national party Podemos and to the Greens and were committed to the public management of their water services. The Madrid party, Ahora Madrid, immediately stopped the privatizing of the city's water. Then in 2016, the Court of Justice of Catalonia sided with Aigua és Vida in its legal challenge, saying the Barcelona concession to Agbar was not justified as it was done without public tender. The case has gone to the Spanish supreme court, where a ruling is expected in 2019.

Barcelona en Comú is the citizens' platform that won the city's municipal election and immediately set to work to challenge the water privatization. A year later, it launched a network of public operators and civil society organizations to support other cities wanting to re-municipalize their water services. In November 2018, Barcelona city council agreed to hold a referendum on the public management of its water and wastewater services, likely to take place in late 2019. Meanwhile, the cities of Valladolid and Terrassa have decided to cancel their private water concession and bring their water services back under public control.

The Blue Planet Project became involved in Spain when its director, Meera Karunananthan, attended a November 2016 meeting of mayors in Madrid. Karunananthan presented the Blue Communities concept, and we both returned in June 2018 for meetings and public events in Madrid and Barcelona that formalized our relationship with the union AEOPAS; it became a Blue Ambassador. Soon after, councillors from Madrid and its suburb Majadahonda proposed that their constituencies become Blue Communities, and both councils voted in favour in the fall of 2018.

At the other end of the country, Cádiz became a Blue Community on November 23, 2018. Part of its commitment is to promote tap water use by distributing glass water carafes to cafés and restaurants throughout the city. And on World Water Day 2019, Medina-Sidonia, also in Cádiz, Xàbia in Valencia, and Móstoles near Madrid all became proud Blue Communities.

Germany

Back in 1994, Berlin set the stage for the commercialization of its water system, Berliner Wasserbetriebe (BWB), by requiring the public company to operate as if it were a private one. Five years later, the city sold 49.9% of BWB to the private German water company RWE Aqua and Veolia. Despite their minority share, the private water companies controlled the management and were guaranteed high profits through secret contracts, according to Transnational Institute's researcher Philipp Terhorst in a June 2014 report called *Re-municipalization in Berlin After the Buy-back*. For 30 years, this public-private partnership couldn't be cancelled or renegotiated and, as a result, Berlin saw a rapid rise in water prices, massive sector layoffs and a reduction in infrastructure investment. From a perspective of democracy, social good and the water infrastructure, the commercialization of Berlin's water company was a disaster, says the institute, but from the perspective of the companies' shareholders, it was a windfall.

Frustrated with the lack of transparency and the steadily rising water rates, a group of activists in the city set up the Berlin Water Table in 2006. Their logo, which became famous, was a shark holding a water faucet in its jaws. The group launched a referendum to force the disclosure of the secret contracts. In February 2011, 666,235 Berliners voted in favour of the proposition "No more secret contracts. Berliners want their water back" — it was a huge victory. The Berlin Senate was forced to act on re-municipalizing the water system and had to buy back the water company. It cost almost US$1.5 billion and was financed by a 30-year taxpayer loan.

Not content to leave it there, pro-democracy groups rallied to have Berlin declared a Blue Community to ensure that water privatization would never happen again. Dorothea Harlin was one of the founders of the Berlin Water Table and a driving force in the fight for water justice. She tells of a small group of volunteers who worked for more than a decade to bring the issue to public attention. "No topic moves people as much as water," she says. "We hardly had to justify to ordinary people why water should not be privatized. We ourselves consist of about 70% water and there is no life on this planet without water."

Harlin teamed up with Christa Hecht, then with the German Association of Public Water Operators. I visited Germany several times and presented the Blue Community proposal to the Berlin Parliament in 2017. So, it was a great pleasure to stand under a tent in the pouring rain with Harlin, Hecht and city officials to celebrate this milestone in October 2018. Several days before, Munich had also become a Blue Community, the result of years of lobbying by water activists there, led by Christiane Hansen with Attac München. The certificate signing and ceremony was held in front of a large and enthusiastic crowd on a stage at the famous Marienplatz where a dark part of the country's history had been born. It was particularly moving to stand with Munich mayor Dieter Reiter as he pledged to fight for justice and support the human right to water for everyone in the world. The day after Berlin, the lovely old city of Augsburg joined them. They all followed Marburg, the first to become a German Blue Community in July 2018.

All of the German Blue Communities joined in Bern's fourth principle: to promote public-public partnerships in the global South. They plan to share their expertise and technology with the communities they work with in the developing world, rather than promote the interests of private European water companies. Karin Brahms, with Marburg's public water works and a leading force behind that city's decision to become a Blue Community, reports that at the 2019 New Year's reception — a highly anticipated event every year — Marburg's mayor, Dr. Thomas Spies, proudly served tap water to the more than 1,000 guests for the first time. They also received Blue Community handbooks and a map with the locations of all their safe drinking fountains in the city.

Munich and Berlin are setting up hundreds of public water refill stations, and Berlin set aside a million euros to implement its Blue Communities commitment. Berlin also resolved to educate the public on the human right to water and what it means that the city has become a Blue Community. It studied its water footprint and to what extent German officials should consider the impact virtual water imports has on the countries of the South with whom they trade when assessing procurement policy. This is an innovative and progressive position to take, as it expresses concern about the environmental and human implications of Germany's trade agreements with poorer countries.

Christa Hecht is convinced there will be more Blue German cities in the future. "Self-regulation is better than compulsion from above," she explains, "as it sets a discussion process in motion and is reviewed on the basis of one's own responsibility." Where once her organization was ridiculed for promoting public water, and the decision to re-municipalize the city's water was controversial, the recent decision to become a Blue Community was not. In fact, it was broadly supported by all the parliamentary groups in the House of Representatives.

Great Britain and Ireland

As their water services were privatized in the 1980s, there are no Blue Communities in England and Wales. (Scotland's water escaped the privatization trend and is still is run by a public water company.) The push to reopen this debate has begun in England. In May 2017, weeks after a media story about Thames Water being fined more than US$25 million for pumping almost two billion litres of raw sewage into the Thames River, Labour leader Jeremy Corbyn promised to bring water services back under public ownership if and when his party forms the government.

By September 2018, the Labour Party had committed to a new report called *Clear Water: Labour's Vision for a Modern and Transparent Publicly-Owned Water System.* Noting that water bills had increased 40% under privatization and that the private water companies had paid out almost US$23 billion in dividends to shareholders in the last ten years, the party set out its plan to convert to a "new democratically run, public water company." Even the Conservative party is unhappy: in February 2018, Environment Secretary Michael Gove called for a crackdown on excessive executive pay and the use of offshore tax havens by England's water companies.

In Ireland, hundreds of thousands of protesters took to the streets to stop the government from completing its installation of mandatory water meters in all residences. The water meters were a requisite of the austerity measures set by the Troika in 2010 in exchange for debt relief. Most believed that the new company established to carry out the plan was the first step on the road to water privatization. As in other countries, a powerful coalition formed to resist the privatization plans, an Irish Right2Water organization.

Ireland had used a progressive tax system to finance its water services, but the water company was now told that it had to operate on a full cost-recovery basis. This new system created high water bills that were impossible for many households to sustain. In the famous Irish tradition of boycott — named for Charles Boycott, whose tenants refused to cooperate when, in 1880, he obtained eviction notices for failure to pay their rent — 57% of Irish residents refused to pay their water bills. The new government dropped the project altogether after the general election of April 2016.

Wanting to enshrine the right to water in the Irish constitution, a group of MPs called Independents4Change has proposed a referendum that reads, "The government shall be collectively responsible for the protection, management and maintenance of the public water system. The government shall ensure in the public interest that this resource remains in public ownership and management." In November 2018, Cabinet approved a process to draft a bill based on this proposal. However, as Dr. Rory

Hearne of Maynooth University reports, public-private partnerships in the wastewater and other water systems are proliferating beneath the political radar in Ireland. He says there are now 115 P3s in water treatment plants across 232 sites — a form of "creeping privatization."

Brendan Ogle, one of the driving forces in the creation of Ireland's Right2Water and the anti-meter campaign, is now working with a number of Irish city councils in their efforts to become Blue Communities.

World Council of Churches

With its head office in Geneva, the World Council of Churches (WCC) consists of 350 churches in 120 countries and represents about 590 million Christians. The issue of the human right to water has been a focus for many years for the WCC. At its 2006 assembly, the WCC adopted a statement titled *Water for Life* that called for the recognition and implementation of the human right to water at every level of governance, including in the UN. It also launched the Ecumenical Water Network with the mandate to protect and realize people's access to water around the world, to promote community-based initiatives and solutions to overcome the global water crisis, to protect water as a gift of God and to advocate for water as a human right.

The organization celebrated when the UN recognized the human right to water and sanitation, and it called on nation-states to amend their constitutions to do the same. The WCC also voiced a strong concern that a "diminished understanding of water simply as a commodity that may be sold and traded according to market principles" endangers those who are most vulnerable.

So, it was a natural step for the World Council of Churches itself to become a Blue Community on October 25, 2016. In his remarks at the ceremony, the general secretary, Reverend Dr. Olav Fykse Tveit, said that with this move, the World Council of Churches had brought the voice of faith communities to the global discourse on the human right to water and sanitation. Green Cross — an NGO founded by Mikhail Gorbachev that works internationally to link issues of security, poverty and environmental degradation and that is an important post–Cold War organization influential at the UN — supported the World Council of Churches in this initiative.

Dinesh Suna is the coordinator of the Ecumenical Water Network and the driving force behind the WCC becoming a Blue Community. Suna notes that in faith communities, it is sometimes easier to preach than to practice. So the WCC's move to become a Blue Community was a tangible way to address its belief that water is a gift of God. The Ecumenical Water Network issued an appeal to all its member churches in Europe and North America where tap water is safe to drink, urging them and their congregations to wean themselves off bottled water. Many were inspired to become Blue Communities as well. The WCC also adopted the principle of solidarity with the global South by promoting public-public partnerships in place of water privatization.

WCC officials recently handed out Blue Community reusable water bottles to a number of prominent visiting church leaders, including Pope Francis, Ecumenical Patriarch Bartholomew of the Eastern Orthodox Church and Archbishop of Canterbury Justin Welby. "Before the WCC became a Blue Community, one couldn't even think of giving an ordinary water bottle to such high-profile church leaders in such high-level events," Suna said.

Consensus around the benefits of maintaining water as a public trust is growing. When these influential institutions and municipalities take a stand to link the human right to water and the fight against its commodification, they cannot but influence the European Union to do the same in its international aid policies. We must put pressure from below on powerful governments to get them to stop promoting water privatization in the global South — and around the world.

CHAPTER FIVE

Going Blue —
One Community at a Time

The number of people now living in Blue Community municipalities exceeds 15 million. This is a significant achievement in ten short years, but much more needs to be done. This project has to grow in other parts of the world, such as the global South. But it still has many more towns and cities to win over and it must also expand its institutional base — universities and schools, faith-based communities, NGOs, unions and community associations. The awareness of our collective responsibility to protect the planet's freshwater and share it more justly needs to grow, as must the understanding of the need to take action. This is where you come in, dear reader. Anyone, anywhere can work within their own community to make it Blue and to personally become a better water user. Then they can expand out, making others aware of the global water crisis and the human and ecological fallout it brings.

The Blue Communities project gives people and communities a blueprint for action, a way to stand up to the larger forces that are endangering local control and stewardship of their area's water resources. Internationally, the project offers an alternative to the model of globalization that promotes the notion that there is only one economic path for the world. Citizens everywhere see international institutions, such as the World Trade Organization and the World Bank, or even their own governments extolling the virtues of privatization of water and other essential services and resources. I cannot count the times that after a presentation or at a book launch, people have said that they totally agree with me on the global water crisis and its causes and possible solutions, but that they feel helpless to do anything about it. Blue Communities is that opportunity.

Emma Lui is the national water campaigner for the Council of Canadians, and she has been key to the Blue Communities project. She believes that the project is important because it gives communities concrete actions they can take to secure public management and oversight of their water services. "Blue Communities is an empowering project that encourages residents and water lovers to take manageable steps to stand up for water and to ask their municipal councils to do the same. It gives people the opportunity to connect with one another, so that there is an active network of residents and groups in place to defend water from privatization, development projects and policies that threaten communities' water sources," she says.

A local Blue Communities campaign can reach many people who don't follow water issues or even municipal politics. Many people do not know what a public-private partnership is and, in many communities, city councils have voted to adopt one with little or no debate or media coverage. Lui believes that a goal of the project is to educate communities before a private company comes in to manage or operate local water services, so that residents can act as a first line of defence. It also helps to educate municipal staff and elected officials to all aspects of the debate, often for the first time.

A big plus of local Blue Communities campaign is that it is positive. So often we activists are fighting rear-guard actions, opposing yet another hydroelectric dam or energy pipeline or gold mine. In the case of promoting Blue Communities, we get to set a positive vision and fight for something we are *for*, instead of something we are *against*. This is why so many anti–bottled water campaigns on university campuses have been successful, as the students got to promote something positive they could do for the planet. It is this point that Berlin's Christa Hecht made: the fight to bring their city's water services back under public control was divisive and bitter, but the Blue Community project was seen as a way of healing and garnered wide support.

The United States

I think the United States is ready for the Blue Community concept to take root. There is already a strong pro public water services movement in many American communities, often led by Food & Water Watch and its dynamic executive director Wenonah Hauter. Atlanta, Georgia, was one of the first American cities to try water privatization in 1999. The city leased its water contract to United Water, a subsidiary of Suez, but city officials soon complained about high water rates, breakdowns, an epidemic of water-main breaks and some "boil-only" alerts caused by brown water pouring from city taps. A mere four years later, Atlanta broke its contract with United Water. In 2003, the city of Stockton, California, contracted with OMI-Thames Water for water services in the face of stiff public opposition, only to also break its contract four years later after a court ruled that the city had used an illegal process in awarding the contract. In November 2018, Baltimore, Maryland, became the first major American city to ban water privatization outright.

While these cities returned to public water services management, they are not Blue Communities. There is still just one Blue Community in the United States: Northampton, Massachusetts. In June 2017, the city council of this city of just over 28,000 people approved a proposal of council president Bill Dwight to become a Blue Community. The idea was the brainchild of Bill Diamond, a professor emeritus at the University of Massachusetts in Amherst. Bill attended a folk festival in Lunenburg, Nova Scotia, in the summer of 2015 where he met members of the local Council of Canadians chapter and heard about the Blue Community campaign. He was amazed that with hundreds of people attending an open-air concert, there were only a handful of plastic bottles left on the ground. Long interested in ways to get people to stop drinking bottled water, he rallied his community and, in particular, the local high school, and many merchants in his town agreed to stop selling bottled water.

Councillor Dwight declared that this was "step one" in changing the way people think about water. His resolution pledged to launch a public awareness campaign to get the public behind the project and set up a task force to follow its progress. It also called upon the state government as trustee of the local watersheds to "apply public trust principles to guide long-term natural resource stewardship and management, and to protect the paramount interests of the public over those of private entities for current and future generations." Further, the city of Northampton called upon the government of the United States to develop a national plan of action to implement the human rights to water and sanitation. Can you imagine if hundreds or thousands of American towns and cities were to follow suit?

The human right to water can never be realized if water services continue to be denied to those Americans who cannot afford rising water rates. Many U.S. cities experience water cut-offs, but none more infamous than Detroit, Michigan, which cut water services to an estimated 250,000 residents in nearly 95,000 households between 2014 and 2017 alone. Another 17,000 households were slated for cut-offs in 2018. After the flight of population and money with the auto industry contraction of the 1980s and '90s, inner-city Detroit found itself without a large enough tax base to provide residents with water services, so it dramatically increased water rates — 400% between 1994 and 2014. Eighty percent of the remaining population is Black and suffers from very high rates of poverty and unemployment. Suddenly, thousands of households found themselves unable to pay their water bills. Private contractors send in crews to cut their water, usually early in the morning, often without warning and sometimes hitting whole blocks at once. Families are left scrambling to find water sources to bathe their children, flush their toilets and cook their meals. Meanwhile, city businesses, golf courses and resorts who did not pay their water bills are not touched.

I visited Detroit many times, meeting with the powerful network of civil rights, water justice, welfare rights and environmental activists who came together to form the Detroit People's Water Board. It struck me immediately that not only was this dreadful practice environmental racism, it violated one of the three obligations governments undertook when they endorsed the UN resolution on the human right to water. The Obligation to Respect very clearly states that a government cannot interfere with a right already granted. We called on the UN to intervene, and three UN special rapporteurs — on water, housing and food — visited Detroit in 2014, examined the evidence and reported that the "unprecedented scale" of the cut-offs violated the human rights of the residents of Detroit.

Detroit and other cities suffering from systemic water cut-offs would be wonderful candidates for Blue Community status. In promising to protect and promote the human right to water, a Blue Community could never cut the water of those who cannot pay their water rates. In late March 2019, Michigan Democrats introduced several bills to guarantee water access for the state's poor. They would create a statewide water affordability program to replace the current patchwork system where each municipality has the authority to offer its own programs or not. They would also institute water shut-off protections for specific vulnerable groups and require clear advance notices of concern in order to help residents come up with a payment plan where possible. A Blue Community campaign could be the spark to deal with this terrible situation and give hope to the thousands in Detroit and around the country still without running water or sanitation.

The Great Lakes–St. Lawrence River Basin forms the largest system of freshwater lakes and rivers in the world, holding more than 20% of the Earth's surface freshwater and 95% of North America's. Yet many residents are concerned about the impact of the plastics crisis on the lakes, and they want to make sure that public control over access to the watershed is maintained. In a thirsty world, there are going to be many demands on the waters of the Great Lakes, and the people who live by its shores have a huge responsibility to act as their stewards. Since 2008, community groups, water advocates and residents have been working to designate the Great Lakes and its tributary waters as a lived commons to be shared, protected, sustainably managed and enjoyed by all who live around them. They have created the Great Lakes Commons Charter Declaration that has been translated into five languages — English, Spanish, French, Kanyen'kéha and Anishinaabemowin — and endorsed by many organizations and First Nations. The basin needs to be protected by a legal, policy, scientific and political framework based on the principles of the public trust doctrine. If the communities that ring the lakes become Blue Communities, these precious waters will have another layer of protection.

FLOW for Water is a Traverse City, Michigan, organization dedicated to the protection of the Great Lakes. Its founder, lawyer Jim Olson, executive director Liz Kirkwood and their team believe that the enduring idea of the commons and the legal principles of public trust can offer unifying adaptive solutions to address systemic basin-wide threats to the Great Lakes. These threats will include increased water conflicts, diversions and climate change impacts.

FLOW and the Council of Canadians together wrote a sample resolution (found at the end of this book) that includes the principle that water is a shared public commons held in trust by each municipality for the health, safety, general welfare and benefit of its residents and citizens, in addition to the other three tenets of a Blue Community. The resolution posits that protecting water as a shared commons will build community resilience and enhance coordinated adaptation to climate change effects and its ecological and human impacts. If momentum were to build among grassroots groups and communities, the pressure to respond to their constituents' concerns would be a powerful incentive to higher levels of government.

Brazil

There is one Blue Community in Brazil, the spa town of Cambuquira in the state of Minas Gerais. São Lourenço is another spa town not far from Cambuquira, one of four founded in the late 19th century after mineral water sources with strong medicinal properties were discovered there. The towns became renowned for their healing waters and people came from all over the country to "take the waters" and enjoy the beauty of the countryside, making tourism an important part of the local economy. In the 1970s, the French company Perrier bought São Lourenço's water park and modernized its local bottled water facility. In 1992, Nestlé bought Perrier and took control of the plant. Several years later, Nestlé dug a new 150-metre-deep well and built a massive new bottled water plant inside the São Lourenço water park, where it started bottling its new brand, Pure Life. Soon, it was pumping 53,000 litres of the park's mineral water every hour and both the flow and quality of the mineral water declined.

Local citizens took the company to court and it was ordered to stop bottling mineral water at the park in 2005. To comply, Nestlé continued to pump and bottle the water but stopped de-mineralizing it, a process banned in the state as it changes the chemical composition of the water left behind. Nestlé critic Franklin Frederick lived in the community at the time, working with the National Conference of Brazilian Bishops. He alerted them to the community concerns and they worked with the Reformed Church in Switzerland, where Nestlé is headquartered, to put pressure on the company. News that Nestlé was looking to buy up water sources in the other spa towns, including theirs, led the citizens of Cambuquira to seek Franklin's help. He suggested they become a Blue Community to prevent their water from being commodified. In June 2014, I visited the community and while there tasted the waters of a number of Cambuquira's water spas, which were stunning in their beauty and serenity. I also toured the São Lourenço water park that had a sour smell and was dominated by the Nestlé bottling plant. The contrast between the two towns was startling.

On a sunny, birdsong-filled June 7, 2014, in the local community centre with its windows open to the air and gardens, Cambuquira became a Blue Community. There was much music and laughter and a few tears. Helber Borges, a young activist who had picked me up at the airport in São Paulo for the five-hour drive on a hot, dirty and crowded highway to Cambuquira, wept openly, tears streaming down his face. "Oh, Maoudee Maoudee" (as he pronounced my name) "I have emotions," he said. Through my own tears, I told him I could see that. In a lovely gesture, Bern Mayor Tschäppät wrote to Cambuquira Mayor Evanderson Xavier to congratulate him and to express solidarity: "I am confident that other communities in Latin America and Europe will soon follow the lead of Cambuquira and Bern. Because if we want to protect the water commons in the face of increasing pressure to privatize water services, it is necessary to build a worldwide network of Blue Communities."

A month later, the Brazilian health authority banned the sale of Nestlé's bottled water from its São Lourenço plant, citing bacterial contamination. Two years later, under increased pressure to close, the company moved its Pure Life production to another location in Brazil and then, in March 2018, sold all its mineral water brands to a Brazilian water company. But Nestlé still owns the water park in São Lourenço and has permitted another company to keep bottling water there. The protests continue. On World Water Day 2018, 600 rural women occupied the plant for days. As Franklin says, "Keep in mind there are four water parks in the region, all with pristine, excellent mineral water sources — a target for the private bottled water sector. They will come, no doubt about it."

The future for water and human rights in Brazil is under dire threat with the 2019 election of Jair Bolsonaro as president. He is unapologetic about his admiration for the country's former military dictatorship, is pro resource extraction and has declared war on Brazil's Indigenous Peoples and their territory, including their forests and water. As reported by Indian geostrategist and author Brahma Chellaney in a January 2019 *Globe and Mail* op-ed, Bolsonaro has vowed to open up the Amazon rainforest to developers by repealing constitutional safeguards for Indigenous lands. Over the last five centuries, reports Chellaney, the number of Indigenous people in Brazil has shrunk from as many as five million to less than a million. Already, the destruction of the Amazon has caused climate disaster, reports leading Brazilian scientist Antonio Donato Nobre. He says that the clear-cutting of the rainforest led directly to the lethal droughts of 2014–2017 in the south of the country, as moisture carried in airborne currents or "flying rivers" was no longer sufficient to bring needed rain.

Bolsonaro must be opposed at home, as well as internationally. But trying to reason with him over his stated intentions would be like trying to reason with American president Donald Trump over his decision to put a known climate denier in charge of the Environmental Protection Agency and slash freshwater protections, as he has done. The rise of these right-wing "strong men" in these and other countries is a compelling argument for local action and for making a difference where one lives and works. A Blue Communities campaign in Brazil would act as a powerful antidote from below to counter the havoc Bolsonaro plans to wreak on his people and the environment.

Vulnerable Communities

Indigenous Peoples are endangered, and not just in Brazil. Chellaney reports that Indigenous Peoples have shrunk to just 4.5% of the global population. They routinely battle mining interests, dam builders, oil-palm plantations, loggers, ranchers, hunters, evangelists and military forces in a desperate attempt to protect their traditional lands and lifeways. In 2007, the United Nations ratified the United Nations Universal Declaration on the Rights of Indigenous Peoples that recognizes that inherent rights include social, cultural, community, spiritual and traditional knowledge. It also recognizes Indigenous protection of natural resources on traditional territory and requires "free, prior and informed consent" for any resource project affecting the local community.

Around the world, Blue Community projects could strengthen the inherent right to water and sanitation of Indigenous Peoples by helping to protect their water resources from exploitation by bottled water companies, mining operations and private utilities. Local Indigenous and peasant groups could form Blue Community networks with others to fight the commodification of their water sources. And Blue Community municipalities and faith-based groups could see advocating for the rights of local Indigenous communities as part of their promise to protect and promote the human right to water and sanitation.

It has been my fervent hope since the United Nations recognized the human rights to water and sanitation in 2010, that more communities and groups fighting for water justice would use that victory in their campaigns. How better to make this resolution real than if we assert our rights from the ground up? In some cities, a Blue Community resolution could be added to protect the rights of undocumented migrants or slum dwellers.

In Berlin, I met a brilliant young man who designed eco-friendly, safe and waterless toilets as part of his contribution to the Blue Community commitment. Sven Riesbeck and his city have teamed up to install these toilets in areas where there are homeless people and migrants, as well as in the red-light district so that sex workers can have a safe place to use a bathroom. His project is spreading to other cities in Germany, and he and his father are installing dry-toilets in India and Ghana. Asked about his reason for putting such energy into this project, Sven says, "Every human being has the right to use a clean toilet for free. As well, we need to save drinking water. So why do we use water to flush human excreta into the river and pollute our natural resources? And why do 2.5 billion not have access to toilets? Dry sanitation is a cost-effective solution for many people in the world who are not able to access clean toilets. By closing the water loop, we are also able to reuse our own nutrients as compost for agriculture and save water."

Marginalized and racialized communities are also taking action, organizing at a grassroots level to force their national governments to take action. Blue Planet Project organizers Meera Karunananthan and Koni Benson facilitated a series of roundtables in South Africa in the fall of 2018 to deal with the water shortage crisis in Cape Town. Karunananthan notes that South Africa is at a crossroads: communities facing the fallout from water scarcity and climate crises are colliding with a neo-liberal state propelled by international financial institutions to facilitate corporate water grabs. The roundtables included front-line activists, academics and representatives of an array of local justice organizations who mapped out a water justice strategy that unites rural and urban water struggles in South Africa. They will use this strategy to offer concrete alternatives for a people-driven, national water justice plan for South Africa.

Many African countries are embracing public-private partnerships, urged to do so by the World Bank, the African Development Bank and even the UN. In a 2017 special publication on Africa called *Partnerships Giving Africa a New Look*, the United Nations Department of Public Information touts global private investment in all levels of public services as the key to a "new" Africa. The Africa-EU Water Partnership Project was set up to achieve the Africa Water Vision for 2025 (the primary political instrument guiding future pan-African water policy) and to help deliver the UN's Millennium Development Goals. The EU has committed to "making more public and private capital accessible for water-related infrastructure projects in Africa" through this vehicle. In other words, it's promoting public-private partnerships.

In the summer of 2018, the South African government announced its intention to lay off 30,000 public sector workers and privatize a number of state-owned enterprises. Many residents of South Africa's townships still have to walk kilometres to find water and they still must use buckets as toilets. It is not lost on them that while apartheid may formally be over, it lives on in their day-to-day lives. Governments that bring in the private sector to invest in water services will guarantee the continued class and race divisions of the past, as the increased prices for essential services will only be accessible to those with a higher income.

Other national governments are also committed to imposing public-private partnerships on their people. In December 2018, Japan's government enacted a revised Water Supply Act that promotes the introduction of a private water concession system in that country's water supply services. The two major public sector unions opposed the bill, saying it was clearly intended to lead to public-private partnerships to run the country's water services. In a strongly worded statement, one of the unions, ZENSUIDO, bemoaned the lack of public consultation and noted the behind-the-scenes involvement of Veolia, whose Japanese affiliate worked closely with government to craft the new law. Takeo Nikaido, the union president, said that municipal waterworks constitute an infrastructure that is public in nature and indispensable to civic life. He pointed out the pride his members have that they have continued to deliver safe, clean water in spite of the fact that their numbers have declined over the past 40 years from 76,000 to 45,000 workers. He also noted that Japan has had many terrible disasters in recent years and that his members have much experience in serving the public in the aftermath.

But it appears the government will not be moved. The only good news in this situation is that the new law is to be implemented at the municipal level and this presents an opportunity to set up a counter-offensive. In an April 2019 poll of local officials, the strong majority opposed the privatization of water services and only 1% responded that they were considering including private concession contracts. Japan's citizens could protect their public water services by setting up committees to lobby their municipal governments to become Blue Communities, thus heading off privatization before it is imposed.

Getting started

The best way to get a Blue Community process started in a municipality is to have a group of residents approach their city council or city officials with the idea. Sometimes, as in the case of Berlin, the network already exists, having fought privatization or another water-related issue, perhaps linked to pollution of a local water source. Often it is the union of water workers that starts the process, but it is very important that any coalition or network working to promote Blue Communities be as broad as possible. If the process starts with a community group, it is essential to involve public sector workers as much as possible. In some cases, as with Bern and Paris, the impetus comes from the top — the mayor or city council itself — though that is rare. Generally, it comes from the grassroots, and the wider the reach, the better. It is important to come armed with documents and sample resolutions. I have included several samples in the appendix. I've also included a sample letter that Blue Communities can use to lobby their state, provincial and federal governments for a plan of action to implement the human rights to water and sanitation at higher levels of government.

A similar process is needed for educational institutions looking to join the Blue Community. The initial impetus might come from a group of students or the student union, or it might be started by teachers and professors. It might grow from some other campus action, such as an anti–bottled water campaign. However it begins, it is critical to hold public campus events to discuss and debate the ideas and actions that might be taken. We are often fighting secrecy and a lack of transparency on the part of private water interests and sometimes even government. It is crucial that we debate openly and show that we have only the best interests of humanity and the planet at heart.

Once the school initiative has begun, it is good to have some concrete plans for what the institution might do to meet its Blue Community commitments. These might include installing accessible water refill stations and hosting onsite lectures about the global water crisis and what ordinary people are doing to address it.

I was at one university in California that held a water awareness week, which involved numerous departments. The history department had students study the historical and sociological aspects of humans and water. Biology and chemistry published materials to help non-biochem students understand basic water science. Environment and sustainability profs and students held panels on water pollution and climate change. Human rights groups presented the issues of race, class and gender in addressing water access. The music department wrote a beautiful symphony to water. English lit students held a fiction contest centred on the theme of water. It was exhilarating.

Members of a faith-based congregation can approach their church leaders about becoming a Blue Community. The initiative could be linked to human rights and anti-poverty work the congregation may already be engaged in. Many faith-based groups are deeply committed to ecojustice or, as the World Council of Churches puts it, "our proper relationship as people of faith to God's creation and to each other, given our utter and complete dependence on the ecological integrity of the Earth." Pope Francis declared access to safe drinkable water to be a basic universal human right in his 2015 Encyclical, in which he mentioned climate change 12 times but water 47 times. Patriarch Bartholomew of the Eastern Orthodox Church extolled both the work on the human right to water and the importance of the Blue Communities project at a speech he delivered to the World Council of Churches in Geneva on April 24, 2017.

While these are important and exciting inroads given the sheer numbers of people these churches can reach, it is crucial that the Blue Communities movement move beyond the Christian churches to be adopted by other faiths.

I remember one international campaign in the late 1990s against a particularly pernicious free trade agreement called the Multilateral Agreement on Investment (MAI). We were successful in defeating it, not least by taking the campaign to the grassroots levels. In Canada, not only did we get dozens of municipalities to adopt MAI-free zone resolutions, but we got into smaller jurisdictions as well. We had libraries and seniors' residences and local community centres proudly displaying stickers and handing out information on the deal to anyone who walked through their doors. By my count, there were more than 600 MAI-free zones in Canada alone when the governments pulled the plug on the deal.

It helps if there is a central organization or a network to oversee the process within a country. In Canada, this has been the Council of Canadians, the Canadian Union of Public Employees and Eau Secours. Our local activists have generally been the ones who take up the issue with their municipalities. In Switzerland, it is the Reformed Church and its Blue Communities coordinator Lisa Krebs. In Germany, it has been Christa Hecht through her association of public water operators. At the international level, the Blue Planet Project coordinates Blue Communities and dispenses the certificates.

We are encouraging people or organizations to work with us to promote our dream in their own constituency or community, calling them our Blue Community Ambassadors. I was invited to Stockholm, Sweden, in December 2018 to speak on water issues as part of the Nobel Prize week events. There I met with the wonderful people of the Right Livelihood Award — the "Alternative Nobel" — who have offered their organization as a Blue Community Ambassador, spreading the word among their vast community of influential social justice and human rights activists.

It is clear that the next step in our work must be to continue to connect these various Blue Community groups and Ambassadors for they have tremendous potential to build common cause around the world.

AFTERWORD

Dreaming a Great Dream

I have spent most of my adult life learning about water and worrying about what we humans are doing to it. I have experienced many downs and some very wonderful ups. I have never discovered any more powerful truth than this: the world will only be transformed from the bottom up, from people fighting in their own communities because they care. Or as Food & Water Watch's motto says, "Fight like you live here." The world needs a new water ethic where all we do — all policy we create, the way we produce energy and trade across borders and grow our food — must ask the question: what is the impact on water and on water justice? And if the answer is in the negative, we must go back and begin again. To know what really works and what does not, we must go to the grassroots. No one knows the local situation like the people who live in and love their community, and it is to them we must turn to save the world's water.

Emma Lui hopes that the Blue Community project going global will provide an opportunity to educate people on the traditional Indigenous lands on which they live and the rights of the first peoples to local waterways. She says that coming together to protect water forms bonds that cut across distance, age, upbringing and diverse backgrounds and presents a new opportunity for collaboration and solidarity. Meera Karunananthan says she hopes that Blue Communities will not be seen in isolation but become part of a larger process to reclaim cities from the excesses of neo-liberal capitalism in order to make them work for the people who built and live in them. The provision of safe, clean public water and sanitation services for all without discrimination is fundamental to ensuring people are able to live healthy, safe and dignified lives.

On this tenth anniversary of the launch of the Blue Communities project, it is my hope and my dream that it can unite us in the quest for sound water stewardship and water justice.

ACKNOWLEDGEMENTS

The Blue Community project and this book are the result of the hard work of many people, more than I can name here. I want to thank with all my heart the wonderful water activists around the world. We have created a powerful movement whose time has come, and our fight for water justice cannot be stopped.

I want to thank the team at the Council of Canadians and Leo Broderick and the board for stepping in to let me do this work. In particular, I want to thank Emma Lui, the national water campaigner; Meera Karunananthan, director of the Council's Blue Planet Project; and Pam Woolridge, communications officer, for their help with research and implementing the project itself. My assistant Kathie Cloutier is a rock. Thank you also to Paul Moist and other CUPE friends who launched this dream with us a decade ago, and to Alice-Anne Simard and her team at Eau Secours, who are doing a great job in Quebec. Many other international allies too numerous to name here are found in the pages of this book. I thank you all.

I am deep grateful to Ellen Dorsey and the Wallace Foundation for their financial support of the Blue Planet Project. Thank you again to my brilliant and patient editor, Susan Renouf, and the great team at ECW Press.

And always, Andrew and my family. You make it all worthwhile.

APPENDIX

Sample Documents

It can be daunting to know where to start if you want to help your town or city become a Blue Community. In this section are sample letters and resolutions that other activists have used in their campaigns. They will give you some ideas, and you can use them as a guide when you craft your own letters and resolutions. These are guides and inspirations only. Every community is different, and it's important that your written materials reflect your own community's needs and concerns.

Sample resolution: Recognizing the human rights to water and sanitation

WHEREAS almost two billion people around the world do not have access to clean drinking water, four billion people face severe water scarcity and 2.5 billion people do not have adequate sanitation; and

WHEREAS Indigenous and racialized communities have been disproportionately affected by the lack of access to safe water and sanitation; and

WHEREAS on July 28, 2010, the United Nations General Assembly passed a resolution recognizing the human rights to water and sanitation; and

WHEREAS on September 23, 2011, the United Nations Human Rights Council passed a resolution on the human rights to safe drinking water and sanitation and called on governments to take concrete action by developing plans of action, establishing monitoring and account-ability mechanisms and ensuring affordable services for everyone; and

WHEREAS the human rights to water and sanitation are directly tied to the right to human health recognized by the United Nations; and

WHEREAS recognizing the rights to water and sani-tation is one of three steps needed to declare [name of municipality] a Blue Community;

THEREFORE BE IT RESOLVED that [name of municipality] recognizes and affirms that water and sani-tation are fundamental human rights.

BE IT FURTHER RESOLVED that [name of munici-pality] will refrain from shutting off water and wastewater services in any residence where residents have an inability to pay their bills, and that [name of municipality] will make every effort to work with the resident to remediate the debt.

BE IT FURTHER RESOLVED that [name of munic-ipality] will call on the federal, provincial and state governments to enshrine the human rights to water and sanitation in federal, provincial and state law.

BE IT FURTHER RESOLVED that [name of municipality] will call on the federal government to develop a national plan of action to implement the human rights to water and sanitation.

Sample resolution: Promoting publicly financed, owned and operated safe water and wastewater services

WHEREAS public health depends on equitable access to drinking water and sanitation systems; and

WHEREAS public ownership and operation of drinking water and wastewater treatment systems have been fundamental to access and quality over the past century; and

WHEREAS [name of municipality] is committed to protecting water and wastewater systems from the consequences of privatization through "public-private partnerships," or P3s, including:

- lack of transparency and public accountability;
- increased costs;
- higher user fees;
- multi-decade contracts that limit the policy options of future local governments; and
- international trade deals providing private water companies with rights to sue municipalities that bring water services into public hands; and

WHEREAS the privatization of municipal water and wastewater treatment systems and services through P3s or contracting out turns water into a commodity to be sold for profit; and

WHEREAS the federal government is requiring much-needed improvements to wastewater standards, a situation that could open the door to privatization unless dedicated public infrastructure funding is provided to upgrade treatment facilities; and

WHEREAS keeping water and wastewater infrastructure public is one of three steps needed to declare [name of municipality] a Blue Community;

THEREFORE BE IT RESOLVED that [name of municipality] opposes privatization in any form of water and wastewater treatment infrastructure and services, including through P3s or short-term service contracts, and resolves to keep these services publicly financed, owned, operated and managed; and

BE IT FURTHER RESOLVED that [name of municipality] lobby the federal government to fulfill its responsibility to support municipal infrastructure by investing in a national water and wastewater infrastructure fund that would address the growing need to renew existing water and wastewater infrastructure and build new systems, and that would only fund public projects; and

BE IT FURTHER RESOLVED that [name of municipality] forward this resolution to the national federation

representing municipalities across the country for circulation to its members.

Sample resolution: Banning or phasing out the sale of bottled water in municipal facilities and at municipal events

WHEREAS [name of municipality] operates and main-
tains a regulated and sophisticated water treatment and
distribution system that meets some of the most stringent
water quality requirements in the world; and

WHEREAS the regulatory requirements for monitoring
water quality contained in bottled water are not as stringent as those that must be met by [name of municipality
or community]; and

WHEREAS single-use bottled water is up to 3,000
times more expensive than water from the tap in [name
of municipality], even though bottled water can originate
from municipal water systems; and

WHEREAS resource extraction, packaging and distribution of bottled water creates unnecessary air quality and
climate change impacts, consumes unnecessary resources
such as oil in the manufacturing of plastic bottles and
fuel used in the transportation of bottled water to the
consumer and creates unnecessary recycling and waste
disposal costs; and

WHEREAS [name of municipality]'s tap water is safe,
healthy and accessible to residents and visitors, is readily

available at most indoor public facilities, and is substantially more sustainable than bottled water; and

WHEREAS when access to municipal tap water does not exist, bottled water can be an appropriate alternative;

WHEREAS banning [or phasing out] the sale and provision of bottled water in municipal facilities and at municipal events is one of the three steps needed to declare [name of municipality] a Blue Community;

THEREFORE BE IT RESOLVED THAT, where access to municipal tap water exists, single-use bottled water will no longer be sold in municipal facilities [or will be phased out by (year)], from municipally owned or municipally administered concessions, or from vending machines in public facilities; and

BE IT FURTHER RESOLVED THAT single-use bottled water will no longer be purchased and provided at municipal meetings and events where access to municipal water exists; and

BE IT FURTHER RESOLVED THAT the availability of water jugs with municipal water will be increased at municipally organized meetings and events; and

BE IT FURTHER RESOLVED THAT a staff and public awareness campaign will be developed to support the rationale for these important changes; and

BE IT FURTHER RESOLVED THAT staff develop an implementation schedule with timelines, that includes an assessment of access to tap water at municipal facilities; and

BE IT FURTHER RESOLVED THAT staff provide a progress report at regular intervals.

Sample letter to the federal government

The movement to recognize and uphold the human rights to water and sanitation is spreading from community to community. Yet communities need federal leadership. Blue Communities commit to calling on the federal government to develop a plan of action to implement the human rights to water and sanitation. Once your municipality becomes a Blue Community, your mayor can customize this sample letter and send it to the federal government.

Dear Environment Minister [name of current minister] and Minister of Infrastructure and Communities [name of current minister]:

The municipality of [name of municipality] recently became a Blue Community. A Blue Community is one that adopts a water commons framework by taking three actions:

1. recognizing water and sanitation as human rights;
2. promoting publicly financed, owned and operated water and wastewater services; and
3. banning the sale of bottled water in public facilities and at municipal events.

A water commons framework treats water as being shared by everyone, and the responsibility of all. Water is central to our lives and so it must be governed by principles and policies that allow for reasonable use, equal distribution and responsible treatment in order to preserve it for nature and future generations.

On July 28, 2010, 122 countries overwhelmingly voted to pass a resolution recognizing the human rights to water and sanitation. Since then, the UN Human Rights Council has passed two resolutions calling on governments to develop comprehensive plans and strategies to implement these rights, assess the implementation of the plans of action, ensure affordable water and sanitation services for everyone and create accountability mechanisms and legal remedies.

We applaud the government of [your country] for endorsing the human rights to water and sanitation at the Rio+20 United Nations Conference on Sustainable Development in June 2012. However, to give the resolutions life, we urge the federal government to enshrine water and sanitation as human rights in federal law and develop a plan of action that will implement these rights.

As part of being a Blue Community, our municipality is opposed to the privatization of water and wastewater services, including through public-private partnerships.

We urge you to support municipal infrastructure by investing in a national water and wastewater fund that addresses the growing needs of communities to maintain and strengthen water and wastewater systems. We call on the Government of [your country] to respect the autonomy of municipalities by providing needed infrastructure funding without attaching conditions. The most transparent and cost-effective way to fund infrastructure is to keep it publicly financed, owned and operated. We urge the government to support communities' and municipalities' efforts to keep water and wastewater services public and community-run.

In order to protect our water sources and ensure clean, safe drinking water, we urge the federal government to develop legislation that recognizes the human rights to water and sanitation, establishes national enforceable drinking water standards and invests in public water and wastewater infrastructure in municipalities.

Sincerely,

Sample resolution for Indigenous Blue Community

This resolution was written by and for First Nations communities in Canada but can be adapted to the situation of Indigenous communities in other countries.

WHEREAS almost two billion people around the world do not have access to clean drinking water, four billion people face severe water scarcity and 2.5 billion people do not have adequate sanitation; and

WHEREAS Indigenous communities — First Nations, Métis and Inuit — in Canada have been disproportionately affected by lack of access to safe drinking water and sanitation services; and

WHEREAS the 2011 National Engineering Assessment, a study commissioned by the Canadian government on the condition of First Nations water and wastewater systems, found that 73 percent of water systems were at medium to high risk; and

WHEREAS there are routinely more than 100 water advisories in effect in First Nations where people cannot drink straight from the tap, with half of the communities living under advisories for over five years and a number of communities living under advisories for more than ten years; and

WHEREAS on July 28, 2010, the United Nations General Assembly passed a resolution recognizing the human rights to water and sanitation; and

WHEREAS on September 23, 2011, the United Nations Human Rights Council passed a resolution on the human right to safe drinking water and sanitation and called on governments to take concrete action by:

- developing plans of action;
- establishing monitoring and accountability mechanisms that ensure free, effective, meaningful and non-discriminatory participation of all people and communities;
- ensuring affordable services for everyone; and
- providing a framework of accountability with adequate monitoring mechanisms and legal remedies; and

WHEREAS bottled water is routinely used as an interim measure to lack of access to drinking water in many First Nations, but is not a sustainable or cost-effective solution; and

WHEREAS the Safe Drinking Water for First Nations Act creates necessary, high standards for drinking water but was passed without allocating adequate funding and without free, prior and informed consent of Indigenous communities. These conditions can force Indigenous communities to turn to funding from private companies under the P3 (public-private partnership) Canada fund;

THEREFORE BE IT RESOLVED that [name of Indigenous community] recognizes and affirms that water and sanitation are fundamental human rights; and

BE IT FURTHER RESOLVED that [name of Indigenous community] opposes privatization in any form of water and wastewater treatment services, including through P3s, and will keep these services community owned, operated and delivered; and

BE IT FURTHER RESOLVED that [name of Indigenous community] call upon the federal government to allocate $4.7 billion to water and wastewater infrastructure in First Nations, as called for by the National Engineering Assessment, and make adequate funding available without the condition of a P3 agreement; and

BE IT FURTHER RESOLVED that bottled water will not be sold at any community facilities or events in [name of Indigenous community] where potable water is available; and

BE IT FURTHER RESOLVED that the [name of Indigenous community] Chief and Council forward this resolution to the Assembly of First Nations for circulation to all First Nations; and

BE IT FURTHER RESOLVED that [name of Indigenous community] will call on the federal and provincial governments to enshrine water and sanitation as human rights in federal and provincial law; and

BE IT FURTHER RESOLVED that [name of Indigenous community] will call on the Government of Canada to develop a national plan of action to implement the human rights to water and sanitation.

Sample resolution recognizing the public trust that protects the waters of the Great Lakes

This sample resolution addresses the issues of seeing a watershed as part of a commons to be managed on a watershed basis. It comes from the perspective of the American states that surround the Great Lakes but can serve as a template for watersheds around the world.

WHEREAS the human rights to water and sanitation and the right to human health are recognized by the United Nations and the right to health has been protected by the courts under the United States Constitution;

WHEREAS, waters of the Great Lakes Basin are recognized as a precious water resource held in public trust, meaning water is central to the very existence, health and sustenance of people, plants and animals living on or near them and therefore must be protected for the common good from generation to generation; and

WHEREAS, the Great Lakes represent 20% of the planet's surface freshwater and 95% of the surface freshwater in the United States and is only 1% renewable; and

WHEREAS, the waters and bottomlands of the Great Lakes are held in trust by the eight Great Lake states for use and enjoyment by its current and future citizens. The states, as trustees, have a perpetual responsibility to the public, as beneficiaries, to manage these bottomlands and waters for the prevention of pollution, diminishment or impairment for the protection of the water, natural resources, and to steward the public's fundamental rights of fishing, navigation, commerce, drinking water, hunting, swimming, sustenance, recreation and ecological values; and

WHEREAS, climate change represents the largest water diversion out of the Great Lakes, increases water temperature and water levels, and threatens the security, flows, levels and health of our Great Lakes; and

WHEREAS recognizing the waters of the Great Lakes as a public trust is one of four steps needed to declare [name of municipality] a Blue Community;

THEREFORE BE IT RESOLVED that water is a

shared public commons and public resource held in [public] trust by [name of municipality] for the health, safety, general welfare and benefit of its residents and citizens; that protecting water as a shared public commons will build community resilience and adaption to climate change effects and ecological and human impacts; and that the [municipality] through its decisions and actions will assure its citizens that it will protect the integrity of the natural waters and public water supplies in quality and quantity from adverse pollution, impairment, waste or from transfer or alienation for primarily private (as opposed to public) benefit, or from interference, or control.

BE IT FURTHER RESOLVED that the [municipality] will equally call on the state government, as trustee of the waters of the Great Lakes, to apply public trust principles to guide long-term natural resource stewardship and management, protect the paramount interests of the public over private ones, and uphold public trust law for the protection of these waters and the benefit of current and future generations.

MAUDE BARLOW is the international bestselling author of 19 books, including the bestselling Blue Water trilogy. She is the honorary chair of the Council of Canadians and of the Washington-based Food and Water Watch. She is on the executive committee of the Global Alliance for the Rights of Nature and a councillor with the World Future Council. In 2008–09, she served as senior advisor on water to the 63rd president of the UN General Assembly and was a leader in the campaign to have water recognized as a human right by the UN. In 2005, she won the prestigious Right Livelihood Award, the "alternative Nobel." She lives in Ottawa, Ontario.